JENNIFER WERNER, SECOND PLACE SPOT NEWS, FOURNIER NEWSPAPERS, KENT, WASH

March 27. A warning. May 18. The mountain blew its top. July 22. A dramatic but not so devastating performance. Jennifer Werner read about the early eruptions of Mt. St. Helens and figured she had missed the story of a decade while she was vacationing on the east coast. Werner's editors assigned her to cover the mountain's mid-summer activity and she got this shot on July 22. Even with a second chance, she guessed she was lucky ... two of her three cameras failed while she was trying to get this picture.

Mt. St. Helens rested 123 years before its March eruption, a mere suggestion of the horror to be witnessed less than eight weeks later. Above is a 360° panoramic view of Mt. St. Helens before the blast of May 18, 1980. The photograph was made a month before the explosion. Below is the same view, four months after, from a point approximately 7.5 miles north of Mt. St. Helens. Spirit Lake and thousands of acres of Gifford Pinchot National Forest became portions of the devastating loss. Then came statistics and superlatives. A heyday for writers and photographers. Reporters struggled to describe what the pictures clearly revealed about Mt. St. Helens. From the first announcement by geologists that the swollen side of the mountain was growing five feet per day, to the explosive thunder of power equal to ten megatons of TNT, the event challenged journalists. Printers ran double-time to produce the surge of supplements, special editions, books and posters. Photographers talked of their once-in-a-lifetime opportunity and portfolios grew. Hot mud and gritty ash boiled and blew over land, lakes and dwellings. Mountain-made scenes for the too-real drama of nature vs. humanity tumbled together in an event sufficient to remind us of our smallness; our helplessness in confronting the force of a live volcano.

Among those lost to the rage of Mt. St. Helens was Reid Turner Blackburn, 27, a photographer for The Columbian, Vancouver, Wash. Reid died while trying to photograph the May 18th blast from his camp just eight miles from the spewing crater.

BOTH PHOTOS: MICHAEL LAWTON FOR NATIONAL GEOGRAPHIC MAGAZINE

the best of
Photojournalism/6

An annual based on the 38th Pictures of the Year competition sponsored by the National Press Photographers Association, the University of Missouri School of Journalism supported by an educational grant from Nikon, Inc.

GEORGE ROSE, LOS ANGELES

Veita Jo Hampton, editor

Copyright © 1981
National Press Photographers Association
University of Missouri School of Journalism
Columbia, Missouri 65205

Library of Congress Catalog Card Number
77-81586

Printed and bound in the United States of
America by the Publications Division of
Jostens/American Yearbook Topeka, Kansas
66609

For information concerning
Photojournalism/6 or any book in
this series, contact Charles Cooper,
Executive Director, National Press
Photographers Association
P.O. Box 1146
Durham, NC 27702

For information concerning
Pictures of the Year compeition,
contact
POY Director
University of Missouri School of
Journalism
Columbia, MO 65205

ISBN 0-930552-05-9

COVER PHOTOGRAPH: (title)
"Intimate Meeting" James
Ruebsamen was one of 200
members of the press invited to
visit the Reagans at their ranch in
the hills north of Santa Barbara,
prior to Ronald Reagan becoming
President of the United States.
(Pictures from the same event: pp
62-63)

JAMES RUEBSAMEN, FIRST PLACE CAMPAIGN '80,
SANTA MONICA EVENING OUTLOOK

A UPI photographer rushes away
from fire that burned hundreds of
acres near the borders of Orange
and Riverside counties in
California.

the best of

Photojournalism/6

Contents

OVERLEAF: (left)
A sailboat drifts through the fog in San Francisco Bay. It appeared just as the photographer discovered a point from which to view the San Francisco skyline.

GEORGE WEDDING, FIRST PLACE NEWSPAPER PICTORIAL, SAN JOSE MERCURY NEWS

OVERLEAF: (right)
Desalles Church, atop a ridge that overlooks the Ohio River Valley, was photographed at sunrise for the Cincinnati Enquirer magazine.

MICHAEL E. KEATING, FIRST PLACE MAGAZINE PICTORIAL CINCINNATI ENQUIRER MAGAZINE

Borrowing an idea from construction workers who hang sheet rock, a photo-stringer covers President Carter from an elevated vantage point.

JOHN RAOUX, THE LEDGER, LAKELAND, FLA.

the best of

Photojournalism/6

It was a year of violence and compassion. Which pictures will be remembered as the most important images from the events of 1980?

America changed presidents and a Republican moved into the White House. China opened its doors to western visitors and an era of change. There were political executions in Liberia. Independent unions in Poland won the right to strike. Fifty-two American hostages remained in Iran and eight soldiers were killed in the aborted attempt to rescue them. There was rioting in Miami, terror in El Salvador and death by violence throughout the world. John Lennon was murdered outside his New York apartment.

Boatloads of Haitians and Cubans sought refuge and freedom on America's southern shores. Mother Teresa cared for the sick, poor and dying in India and worked to establish missions all over the world.

The Sunshine Skyway bridge fell into Tampa Bay. The first solar-powered flight was recorded. Walter Cronkite retired.

Mud wrestling was a fad. John McEnroe gained fame in smashing performances on the world's tennis courts. Football continued to be a mild form of national hysteria. In bars and living rooms around the country, where television sets were tuned to the Winter Olympics, people went wild as the U.S. Hockey team beat the Soviet team, 4-3, then took a Gold Medal by defeating Finland.

To top it all was the eruption of Mt. St. Helens. Nature may need 300 years to heal the wounds left on the face of the Pacific Northwest. Floods, earthquakes and hurricanes took lives. America's summer drought destroyed lawns and crops and rattled the nation's agricultural economy. Inflation continued.

Following is the work of 176 photographers. There were 77 winners. The additional pictures were selected to compliment the work of the winners and add dimension to this collection which is unavailable in any other form.

On the road to Ban Nam Yao, a refugee camp in mountainous northern Thailand, 20 miles from the Laotian border, this picture was made as part of a series on Milwaukeeans who were working to aid Cambodian and Laotian refugees. To clear the land for planting in early spring, Thais use a method called, "slash and burn." Mountainsides can be seen burning day and night and a smoky haze blankets many miles of countryside.

ERWIN GEBHARD, SECOND PLACE NEWSPAPER PICTORIAL, MILWAUKEE JOURNAL

When viewers see this picture for the first time, they study what appears to be a bright gold blanket, carelessly slung over a desert scene. It takes a minute to realize that the gold blanket is a ripple of giant sand dunes mirrored in the still surface of a lake. Nature journalist and photographer, Uwe George produced 19 such pictures for a GEO article about the oceans under the Sahara. This photograph of Libya's Lake Mandara was used as the lead picture.

Using a 50mm lens and color film with an ASA of 64, Steve McCurry and Lauren Stockbower produced the silhouette of camels, camel herders, and a sunset cigarette break. In the GEO article with which this picture appeared, camels were criticized and complimented, establishing that the behavior of camels is unpredictable.

STEVE MCCURRY & LAUREN STOCKBOWER FOR GEO MAGAZINE, THIRD PLACE PICTORIAL, MAGAZINE DIVISION

UWE GEORGE FOR GEO MAGAZINE

Timelessness was the quality noted by the judges when they commented on this photograph. Strong elements of composition and its stark, wintery mood made it a winner in the magazine pictorial category. Judges were no more (or less) impressed once they heard that it was Prince Philip driving the four-in-hand toward the Long Walk at Windsor Castle. One spread and the cover were used with this picture in the November, 1980 National Geographic. Although the original photograph is in color, it is one of those pictures that remains equally strong in black and white. Called the symbol of "British majesty and stability," Windsor Castle is now more than 900 years old.

JAMES L. STANFIELD, SECOND PLACE MAGAZINE PICTORIAL, NATIONAL GEOGRAPHIC (ORIGINAL IN COLOR)

Because the photographer used one remarkable piece of architecture to frame another, the judges agreed he had skillfully controlled the element of contrast and made a winning picture. Joel Meyerowitz studied St. Louis, particularly the Arch, with an 8 x 10 view camera, and some of his pictures, now collected in book form, were used by GEO. The steel "gateway to the west" is 630 feet high, was designed by sculpter Eero Saarinen and has become a symbol for new development of downtown St. Louis.

Farmers in Zealand, Denmark, burn off excess straw and stubble because the cost of collecting and transporting it is so excessive. But they burn off those hundreds of acres at a considerable risk. The reported loss of "only one farm" in a day's burning was considered to be "reassuring."

Georg Gerster has made a profession of aerial photography. This picture, with even the smallest detail easily readable, is one of several Gerster produced for a GEO article. The judges remarked that his work is filled with information as well as exciting, crazy-quilt graphics.

SCOTT RUTHERFORD, THIRD PLACE FEATURE PICTURE STORY, HERALD JOURNAL, LOGAN, UTAH

Approaching insects still in a stupor from the night's chill and photographing them was an experience Scott Rutherford describes as "having one hell of a good time." He felt photographing an unusual subject was appreciated by his readers. That, with deadline adrenaline, turned his self-assigned project into a real treat. The pictures were made in one morning, dawn to noon, in a small patch of valley marsh. Lenses he used included a 500mm mirror, a 180mm with extension tube and a 55mm macro. He intends to try similar essays on life in an alfalfa field or an alpine meadow.

KEITH HALE, THIRD PLACE PICTORIAL, CHICAGO SUN-TIMES

TOM KASSER, SECOND PLACE NEWSPAPER PORTFOLIO, SAN BERNARDINO SUN

About six A.M. on a hot, August Saturday, Keith Hale became intrigued by the dense fog hovering over a harbor near downtown Chicago. The boats looked to him like ghost-ships. With a zoom lens he converted his Saturday intrigue into a weather shot for the Sunday edition of the Sun-Times.

The family under the tree had come early to watch a race at California State in San Bernardino. If viewers study this photograph closely, they discover that one of the limbs of the tree is human. What the judges interpreted as a nicely composed, graphic picture has a nearly-hidden bit of humor in it.

In vacant Carmack Church Jean Shifrin found Dewey Coffey eating lunch. Since his retirement from the lumber business, Coffey paints small churches in northwestern Missouri. Coffey, who is 76, said, "One of these days I'm gonna have to quit climbing that 32-foot ladder."

Moonrise over Whitebridge Farm in Marlton, New Jersey took two evenings to line up the barn, cows and moon in the viewfinder just the way Dennis McDonald wanted them to be.

At dawn, a waterman poled his barge through the ice on Chincoteague Bay enroute to check his oyster floats. The temperature was two below zero.

JEAN SHIFRIN, ST. JOSEPH (MO) GAZZETTE

DENNIS MCDONALD, BURLINGTON (NJ) COUNTY TIMES

GEORGE H. COOK, III, THE SUNPAPERS, BALTIMORE

As two tug boats pulled Howard Hughes' mammoth flying boat into the harbor at Long Beach, Tom Kasser was photographing from a helicopter. The Spruce Goose had been in a hanger and away from public view since its first and only test flight in 1947. When the City of Long Beach decided to build an oil terminal on the site of the hanger, plans were made to chop the birch plane into pieces and distribute them to various museums. Those plans were abandoned when a company decided to build a structure to exhibit the plane on a site near the HMS Queen Mary, another relic that company operates for the City of Long Beach. The Spruce Goose, a special pride of Howard Hughes, was claimed to be the world's largest airplane when it was built.

The Gossamer Penguin used 2,800 solar cells to sail across the desert at Edwards Air Force Base in August, 1980. The world's first solar powered aircraft converted the sun's energy into electricity to run its propeller.

Looking like a creation of Leonardo daVinci, the Penguin flew about 16 miles per hour and was followed closely by two bicycles traveling at the same speed. Project Manager Ray Morgan rode one bicycle; on the other was photographer Frank Niemeir carrying two cameras so that he could shoot in color and black and white.

Niemeir explained that he would plop the bike down on the dry lake bed, lay down for the needed angle, then hop on and race off to catch up again. Niemeir was pleased that he managed to tie in the sun with the solar powered flight but felt there was only one frame that worked the way he had hoped it would.

In its Sunday, August 7th edition, the Simi Valley Enterprise published a color front, then on August 10th, followed it up with a picture page on which this photograph was printed full width. "I was surprised that UPI didn't want to carry any of my photos that I drove to their L.A. office prior to the official flight, and that TIME magazine didn't even use a story, let alone a photo, on the Penguin. The flight of the Penguin should have had the coverage that the Space Shuttle received."

On the faces of Mt. Rushmore is no place for an acrophobic photographer. Bruce Bisping gathered up his nerve and his cameras, rode a safety seat over the top and dangled among the noses for pictures used with a story on the grooming of Mt. Rushmore. Every fall, park rangers climb over, clean, inspect and repair the national monument. George Washington, Thomas Jefferson, Abraham

Lincoln and Theodore Roosevelt were immortalized by the sculpture in granite that took artist Gutzon Borglum 14 years, (1927-1941), to produce. Cracks are filled with a putty-like mixture of white lead, linseed oil and dust that comes from the granite carved out of the mountain. The filling keeps moisture from seeping in and breaking down the granite.

Scotch, a 23-pound tabby, won the Fattest Cat Contest in Gainesville. The purpose of the show was to raise money for a storefront pet-shop adoption agency that the Humane Society was attempting to open.

Sometimes two in a tub is a crowd. SPCA mascot, Stonewall, shares his bathwater with a pet Mallard.

CLAY PETERSON, SALINAS (CA) CALIFORNIAN

ALAN BERNER, ARIZONA DAILY STAR (TUCSON)

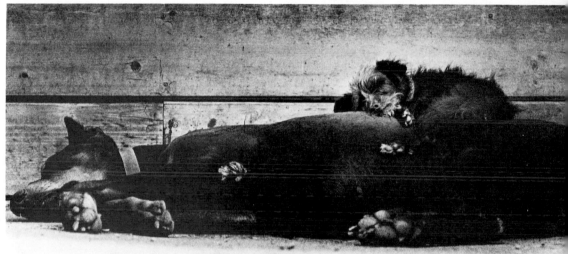

Two dogs dozed through the second annual Bisbee Poetry Festival where the photographer was on assignment.

The question remains as to whether the goat ate or kicked her way through the side of Vern Woolie's goat pen in Missoula, MT. Either way, she is here framed by the damage she has done.

JOHN KAPLAN, GAINESVILLE SUN

RAYMOND K. GEHMAN, THE MISSOULIAN, MISSOULA, MT

A tree blocked the wind-driven snow and gave a jogger a target as he cleared a bench in Fall River's North Park (Mass). In mid-winter, such protected patches of grass are reminders that spring will come again.

Several inches of fresh snow covered the chairs on the patio near where John Freeman went for coffee. He remembered a similar group of chairs at a park in downtown Wichita. He drove to the park and managed to get there before passers-by disturbed the snow.

Once he was an art teacher and a sculptor. Now Bruce J. Berry, is a chimney sweep. Photographer Mike Zerby figured the story on Berry would be another nuts and bolts assignment on how to get a chimney cleaned. He was surprised when Berry, in costume, performed this straight up-and-down jump on the peak of a roof. Berry is a serious sweep however, and worries about the possibility of getting lung cancer from cleaning dirty chimneys because creasote is carcinogenic. He also advises his customers to watch out for fly-by-nighters.

Roberta Burnett persuaded a friend to model, did some fancy cut-and-paste work on a studio shot of the man with the binoculars, then re-photographed the entire piece to produce this illustration. The photograph was used with an article about peeping toms and was printed across six columns.

"Arson, a city's curse," was a series published by the Toledo Blade that used David Cron's photograph as a logo. However, editors decided to use it differently than what is seen here; for the series it was cropped in half and the negative was flopped. The word, "ARSON" was printed over the one-column-width picture. Cron felt the picture made its point anyway.

DAVID CRON, SECOND PLACE EDITORIAL ILLUSTRATION, TOLEDO BLADE

Fighting boredom one night in a hotel room, Louie Psihoyos made this statement expressing his reaction to the assassination of musician John Lennon. He set up the shells, covered a flood light with red gelatin and made what he calls his "anti-gun, anti-nuke" statement, one born out of frustration. When entered in competition, the picture had not yet been published.

ROBERTA BURNETT, THIRD PLACE EDITORIAL ILLUSTRATION, COLUMBIA MISSOURIAN

LOUIE PSIHOYOS, FREELANCE, WASHINGTON, D.C. (ORIGINAL IN COLOR)

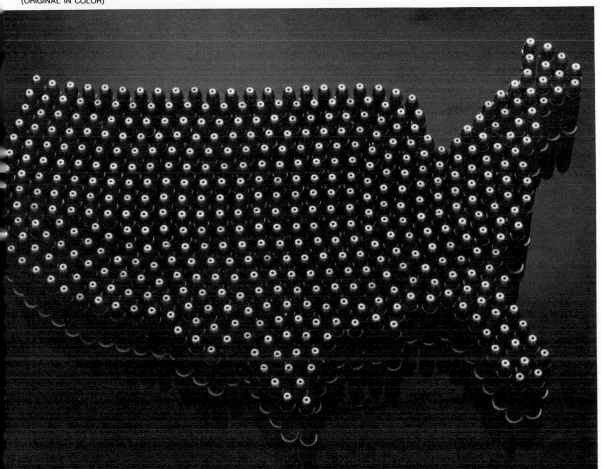

News

Two of the events we expected to happen in 1980 included the national election and the taking of the census. And news photographers did concentrate on the election. But one of the good things about this photojournalism business is that there are always a lot of surprises.

American teams did not attend the Moscow Winter Olympics because we protested Russia's presence in Afghanistan. American bodies were exhibited near wrecked helicopters by Iranian officials who took pleasure in the horror and embarrassment we felt when an attempt to rescue 52 American hostages failed. An American from Texas photographed the execution of 13 Liberian officials, then sneaked film past the authorities and won a Pulitzer for his efforts. Black and white Americans fought each other in the streets of Miami while in the same town, hundreds of Cubans and Haitians arrived hoping to become new Americans. On the other end of the country, Mexicans crossed borders illegally, sustained by the same hope — life would be better in America.

The KKK was active in California and Texas. Murder and threat of murder bloodied streets in cities everywhere. There were fires and accidents, storms and earthquakes. Ships rammed bridges and trains fell off them. And as in each of the past five years, recession, high unemployment and inflation flavored the news.

So we looked for some relief from the pain. We studied Saturn. We watched television. We saw J. R. Ewing get shot and John McEnroe get mad. We learned to love the little green man, Yoda for his gentleness and wisdom, and were equally enchanted with a talking frog and Miss Piggy. People were "into" plants, comic books, contemporary cards with sentimental messages that could be bought at the grocery store. Thirty tons of volcanic ash were sold to those who longed to have a personal keepsake from Mt. Helens' eruption.

The census was taken.

The country-western wave continued. People bought boots and hats and Kenny Rogers or Willie Nelson albums. The fad was so wide-spread that real cowboys had trouble finding "regular and inexpensive" clothes and boots. But we continued to seek relief from the continuous battering of bad news.

That is a good reason to end this news section with the rescue of a cow by helicopter and the exciting conflict between man and bull at a good old-fashioned rodeo. We sometimes wish the news could be all sports, with more fun and less pain.

WERNER GARTUNG, FIRST PLACE MAGAZINE NEWS/DOCUMENTARY FOR LIFE (ORIGINAL IN COLOR).

A revolt in the West African republic of Liberia against a small group of ruling elite, descendants of American slaves, began with the assassination of the 66-year-old president, William R. Tolbert in Monrovia. On April 12, soldiers siezed, shot and disembowled Tolbert. Five days later three others were publicly executed on an Atlantic beach in Monrovia. The execution was intended as a warning to rioters during the first days following the coup d'etat.

Larry Price of the Ft. Worth Star-Telegram was the only American photographer present when 13 Liberian government officials were executed by members of a military coup in the small western African nation. Price was in Liberia because the Ft. Worth Baptist Community maintains an affiliation with the missionary program there. The nation was founded in 1822 by freed American slaves who had established a facsimilie of American constitutional government. That government dissolved into a monarchy in which the people shared very little of the wealth. Price's visit to the missionaries in Liberia just happened to coincide with the assumption of power by the 28-year-old Sgt. Samuel Doe.

At a press conference Doe's representative announced that there would be an execution.

During the shooting, Price was hemmed in by the yelling, cheering crowd and was close enough to be hit above the eye by a shell casing from one of the rifles. (Newsphotographer magazine: June/July 1981) "By bluff and enterprise, Price managed to get his film past the Liberian airport authorities. He substituted exposed film for unexposed in a carefully opened 20-roll pack of Tri-X. Soldiers confiscated his loose film while he carried the exposed rolls out of the country sealed in cellophane in the 'unopened' pack."

STEVE MCCURRY, FREELANCE FOR TIME MAGAZINE
(ORIGINAL IN COLOR)

*In eastern Afghanistan, conflicts grew between the
Soviets and Afghan freedom fighters, who Steve
McCurry photographed in the Kunar Province.
On assignment for TIME, McCurry dressed in the
local garb, dyed his hair and beard, shoe-polished
his face and sneaked past border guards. For four
months he lived with the rebels. "The exciting
part of the assignment was to have witnessed a
popular revolt first-hand," McCurry said. "I often
asked myself why I was there ... those people
were getting shelled and attacked by helicopters.
You can't help getting nervous when there is
shooting. I just tried not to think of the
possibilities."*

The Iraqi Air Force made a direct hit on Abadan's oil refinery, from Soviet-built MiGs. Iranian pilots retaliated in American-made Phantoms and bombed oil storage tanks at an electric power station and a nuclear research center. Black smoke filled the skies over the Persian Gulf and the war between Iran and Iraq continued. The Ayatullah Khomeini promised paradise for all who were killed in battle and Iran's Parliament continued to stall on decisions regarding the fate of 52 American hostages still in Iran. Different frames of this picture were used in TIME and LIFE magazines.

LUCIANO MELLACE, THIRD PLACE GENERAL NEWS, UNITED PRESS INTERNATIONAL

When pictures of faces reflect the tragedy of an event, then photojournalism is successful. "People make news, not things," said one judge.

In the town of Balvano, 150 of 300 persons attending a Sunday night mass were killed when the church roof collapsed during the earthquake in southern Italy.

On November 24, much of the country was rubble. Thousands were dead; 300,000 were homeless. Many died unnecessarily because people in the small towns were unprepared to deal with such disaster.

A child and her grandfather warmed themselves near a fire in a tent at Calabritto, one of the villages leveled by the quake.

GIANNI FOGGIA, ASSOCIATED PRESS

In San Salvador, it was not clear from where the shooting began, from the ruling right or the radical left. Shots rang out among 50,000 people gathered at the funeral of Archbishop Romero who had been assassinated on March 24th. The mourners fled leaving 35 dead. In the aftermath lay crushed bodies, shoes, leaflets and pictures of the archbishop. The cathedral was used as a morgue and stories from the event reported that such violence against the masses was ironic at the funeral for one who strongly condemned violence on any kind.

PATRICK CHAUVEL/SYGMA, FIRST PLACE NEWS PICTURE STORY, MAGAZINE FOR LIFE

Polish workers' leader Lech Walesa (pronounced Vah-wen-sah) before a cheering crowd held up the large pen with which he signed a document obliging the Communist party to legalize independent unions and the right to strike. The agreement came after Gdansk workers walked away from their jobs and threatened collapse of Poland's industrial establishment. There was fear that the Soviet Union would send troops into Poland as it did into Czechoslovakia in 1968.

Lech Walesa was a prime subject for news photographers and writers while the strikes and negotiations continued before a settlement in late summer. He claimed not to be a speaker but had impressive power over the crowds he addressed. Walesa, 37, married, father of six children and a practicing Roman Catholic was at one point "praying it (the strike) will end tonight." His followers describe him as a leader of courage, dignity and strong political convictions.

PETER MARLOW/MAGNUM. THIRD PLACE MAGAZINE NEWS/DOCUMENTARY FOR LIFE MAGAZINE (ORIGINAL IN COLOR)

The savage regime of Pol Pot forced Cambodia's entire urban population into rural slave-labor camps. From LIFE's article titled, "The Pity and Horror of Cambodia" the situation is described; "Schools and hospitals were closed, religion abolished, machinery banned. Books, music, currency, communication — all were barred in pursuit of a 'pure' classless society. Anyone with an education or a modern skill was killed. Children deemed to be offspring of 'undesirables' were buried alive ... before Pol Pot was driven from power by the Vietnamese in 1979, his regime had been responsible for the deaths of four million Cambodians — fully half the population."

JAY ULLAL/STERN, HAMBURG, WEST GERMANY FOR LIFE MAGAZINE

A patriot drew cheers from fellow Americans in Washington, D.C. when he tormented protesting Iranians by setting fire to a copy of the sacred book of Moslems, the Koran.

A charred body with a helmet lies beside the wreckage of a helicopter lost in the aborted attempt to rescue 52 American hostages from Iran. Military officials cancelled the mission when three of eight helicopters broke down and the risk became too great to continue. Still, eight soldiers died in the attempt. The event gave the Ayatullah Khomeini and Iranian officials another opportunity to take advantage of press coverage. The bodies from the wreckage were collected in plastic bags and exhibited to reporters and photographers.

MOHAMED SAYAD, ASSOCIATED PRESS

We have a great need of men and women ready to make sacrifices that freedom and security require. The eight who gave their lives while attempting to free their fellow Americans from an illegal and intolerable captivity were such individuals. They knew the price that freedom can demand and they were prepared to pay it. They laid down their lives for their countrymen, for their nation's honor and for the principles of justice and civilization. We mourn their loss; we admire their courage; we respect their dedications; and, we reaffirm the principles for which they died.

— President Jimmy Carter

The "Tribute to Eight American Servicemen" was a proclamation by President Jimmy Carter on May 6, 1980. The memorial service was the next day at the Arlington National Cemetery in Virginia. Jim Preston produced the photo essay for "All Hands Magazine" with the purpose of showing something contrary to the negative coverage given the aborted rescue mission.

JIM PRESTON, PH1, FOR ALL HANDS MAGAZINE, USN

IN MEMORIAM

Capt Richard L. Bakke, USAF

Capt Harold L. Lewis, Jr., USAF

Capt Lyn D. McIntosh, USAF

Capt Charles T. McMillan, II, USAF

TSgt Joel C. Mayo, USAF

Sgt John D. Harvey, USMC

SSgt Dewey L. Johnson, USMC

Cpl George N. Holmes, Jr., USMC

PAT CROWE, NEWS-JOURNAL COMPANY, WILMINGTON, DE

GENE PUSKAR, ASSOCIATED PRESS

Flag-waving young men gathered outside the Talleyville, Del. post office to urge other young men to register for the draft. The group is part of an organization called Students in Defense of Our Democratic Society. Pat Crowe was happy that he could get a local story on a national event and have the picture of flag-waver Sam LeCompte appear on the front page.

Some of the 356 flags raised in honor of each day the U.S. hostages had been held in Iran flutter in a stiff breeze at Hillcrest Memorial cemetery in Hermitage, Pa. At the time the picture was made by Gene Puskar, new hope for the hostages' release had risen in debate among members of the Iranian Parliament. Besides the frayed edges of some of the flags and the lone figure walking toward the camera, this picture holds one other interesting detail; there is a Canadian flag near the top right corner of the frame.

Campaign '80

There is probably no more appropriate personality whose picture could appear as a lead to this Campaign '80 section than the man who has explained politics and politicians to us from the tube for at least 32 years. In the Pictures of the Year competition, hundreds of photographers never know how close they come to winning. This photograph of Walter Cronkite, for example, initially went to the "out" category but was recalled by the judges who awarded Richard Derk third place. Judges said they had made a conscious effort not to be intimidated by name personalities, but that selection was very difficult because of the number of such persons in both portrait/personality and the Campaign '80 categories.

When this photograph was made, Cronkite had made it clear that he planned to retire. His famous sign off, "And that's the way it is ..." became an American catch phrase, especially during 1980 as he referred nightly to the number of days the hostages had spent in captivity in Iran. A writer for LIFE magazine said Walter Cronkite is known "for his competitive fury." In Derk's picture Cronkite was caught in an off moment of relaxation during the Illinois Primary reports.

RICHARD DERK, THIRD PLACE PORTRAIT/PERSONALITY, CHICAGO SUN-TIMES

Politicians and photographers both know that a strong gesture and expressive face captures more interest from voters than a studio mug shot. John Connally spoke to a crowd of Republicans during the Illinois primary campaign. John Anderson (right) was known throughout the campaign as an adamant orator and continued his impassioned speech-making right to the end of his unsuccessful bid for the presidency. Repeatedly asked whether he would accept the No. 2 spot, George Bush was quoted in the May, 1980 TIME saying, "No way." In this picture Bush is wearing his own "George Bush for President" button.

THOMAS I. PRICE, RICHMOND NEWSPAPERS

More than once during the campaign for the U.S. presidency, First Lady Rosalynn Carter was "the woman in front of the man ..." a phrase Thomas Price uses for the title of this picture. The photographer said that President Carter's immense presence "over her shoulder did not shadow her ability to handle questions or drive home points that she and her husband believed in." Mrs. Carter was speaking at a Democratic fund-raiser in Richmond when Price made the photograph.

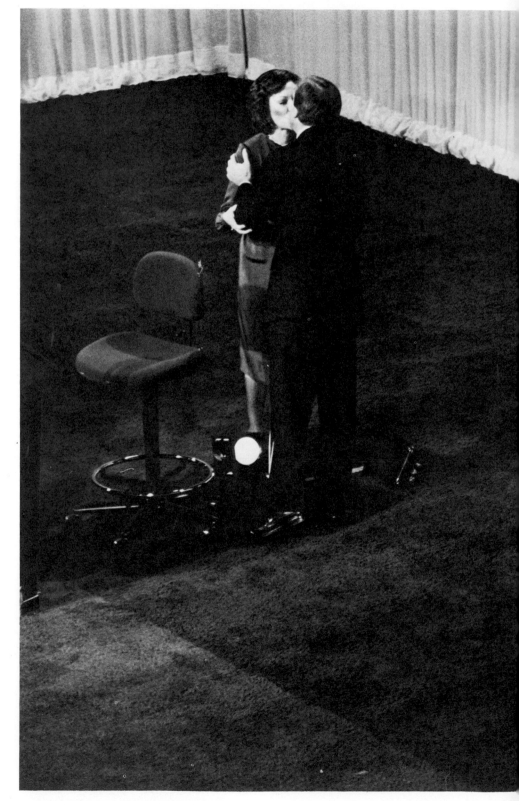

GEORGE WILHELM, THIRD PLACE CAMPAIGN '80,
SIMI VALLEY ENTERPRISE

Judges complimented George Wilhelm and Bob Dougherty for pictures that humanized the candidates. Since the wives figured heavily in the campaign activities, the photograph of the "post-debate-hug-and-kiss" was the kind of summarizing shot the judges were hoping to see. One judge pointed out that the separation of the couples improved the quality of the photograph. The picture of Presidential candidate Ronald Reagan carrying a grocery bag from the butcher shop freezer was again, that human touch with which viewers can identify easily.

BOB DOUGHERTY, SECOND PLACE CAMPAIGN '80, ASSOCIATED PRESS

Nancy and Ron; future First Lady with her husband and President-elect as Reagan delivered a speech at the Los Angeles Times.

MICHAEL EVANS, HONORABLE MENTION CAMPAIGN '80, FOR TIME MAGAZINE
(ORIGINAL IN COLOR)

The newly elected President of the United States and
First Lady photographed by recently appointed White
House photographer, Michael Evans.

Photographer Ann Bailie said, "The event was billed as a photo opportunity and I assumed the only real thing happening would be the media's pursuit of the Reagans." Bailie was correct. However, five of her pictures were used on a page with a story by writer Larry Lynch that described detail-for-detail the events of the day. The Reagans call their special place, the Rancho del Cielo (ranch of the sky) and had invited about 200 members of the press to see Ronald Reagan in jeans and plaid shirt riding a horse along a dusty road. But on this day, Reagan attempted to keep a sense of humor about being jostled and quized by 75 reporters simultaneously, once in a while flashing his former actor's grin at a cameraman or talking about his dog, the horses or the Reagan children. Nancy Reagan appeared to be just "going along for the ride" and reporters noted her sharp replies and protective attitude toward her husband when she occasionally interrupted to give her own answers to reporters' questions.

ANN BAILIE, INDEPENDENT PRESS-TELEGRAM, LONG BEACH, CA

The polls indicated President Jimmy Carter would lose the election. He went home to Plains, Georgia to vote. Fighting back tears and exhaustion as he spoke before supporters at the train depot, Carter said, "I've tried to honor my commitment," then grimacing against emotion," to you. God bless you., Thank you."

Ronald Reagan was contemplating an answer to reporters quizzing him about early returns that showed a three-way tie between himself, George Bush and John Anderson. The truth was more shocking: the final count gave Reagan 489 electoral votes; Carter 49. Only 270 were needed to win. It is noteworthy that there are clusters of tiny horseshoes on his necktie.

GRANT M. HALLER, FIRST PLACE NEWS PICTURE STORY, SEATTLE POST-INTELLIGENCE

May 18. 8:31 a.m. With a power rated 500 times that of the bomb dropped on Hiroshima, Mt. St. Helens blew her top. The ash plume rose 12 miles and by 10 a.m. Grant Haller was near the mountain in a helicopter, trying to understand a new term, "pyroclastic flow." ("flow of fire —")

He made pictures of the boiling ash with a 180mm lens — he knew he was dangerously close to the clouds of steam and debris. Haller said that it is hard to believe what he saw and he is still startled when he looks at his own pictures.

Haller considers himself a hard news junkie and was proud of what photographers achieved while covering the Mt. St. Helens' story. One of his pleasant experiences came after the pictures were finished and he walked through the news room. His colleagues rose and applauded his work. Embarrassing, "but nice . . . ." he said, "very nice."

The most controversial picture to come from the coverage of Mt. St. Helens was that taken from a helicopter by George Wedding. Andy Karr, 11, his brother Mike, 9 and their father died at a camp site 4½ miles west of the mountain on the morning of May 18th. The picture "reduces a monumental geological event to the most elemental vision of human vulnerability," said Chicago Tribune writer James Yuenger. Simply, the mountain killed children and we were unprepared to accept that. Part of the sad result of publication of Wedding's picture was that the family discovered the fate of the boys and their father when their grandfather picked up a newspaper two days after the eruption in Renton, Washington. Meanwhile editors argued as to whether Wedding's picture should be published attempting to guess how readers might react to the particular truth revealed in the photo.

-— continued next page —

GEORGE WEDDING, THIRD PLACE SPOT NEWS, SAN JOSE MERCURY-NEWS

— from page 67 —
Columnists and broadcasters latched on to the emotional impact of the photograph and George Wedding was caught-up in explaining why he took the picture and why journalists make such pictures at all. Andy's mother contacted Wedding and arranged to meet him. She wanted answers . . . he wanted to share his feelings about what was right and wrong in the use and world-wide distribution of the photograph. They walked and talked for more than three hours. What surprised and moved Wedding was the woman's understanding and compassion in spite of her own loss. She wanted to share her memory of Andy and did so by showing pictures of him and his family before the fatal trip to the mountain. There is irony in the story. Andy's father had ignored warnings about camping near the mountain and had circumvented a road block to get to his favorite camp site.

JIM MENDENHALL, COURIER-JOURNAL & LOUISVILLE TIMES

Trees that were 150-feet tall fell like piles of toothpicks from the mighty force of the volcanic blast. Enough lumber was downed, almost instantaneously, to build 30 million three-bedroom homes. A detail that fascinates viewers about this picture is that the timber seems all to have fallen the same direction, like quills layered on the back of a giant porcupine.

GEORGE WEDDING, SAN JOSE MERCURY-NEWS

The explosion and ashfall of Mt. St. Helens killed 60 persons and devastated the Washington countryside with a path eight miles long and 15 miles wide. Searches for victims and survivors conducted by National Guard helicopter crewmen uncovered bodies all along that path. In the coverage of the Mt. St. Helens' story we depended on numerous aerial shots to give us information about what happened. And occasionally, we saw a picture that gave us something of size we could understand. The relationship of helicopter, truck and tree stumps helps us realize the magnitude of our loss.

Twenty persons were injured on an ash-shrouded interstate highway near Centralia, Washington, when 15 cars collided in the northbound lanes. A Centralia fireman aided one victim while another fireman, Joel Hangartner carried an injured child to an ambulance.

The ash-fall from Mt. St. Helens caused many similar accidents. Drivers described their experiences with the gray gritty stuff as something like "driving in a combined sand and snow storm ... when the wind blew you couldn't see throught it ... you couldn't stop quickly and the damn stuff wouldn't melt."

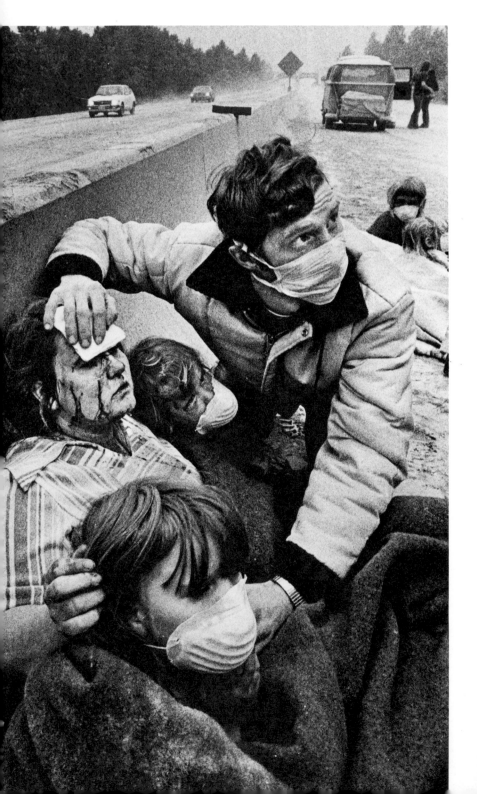

GEORGE WEDDING, FIRST PLACE PORTFOLIO, SAN JOSE MERCURY-NEWS

The Miami area has a population of more than 230,000 blacks. Not since 1967 and the riots in Detroit has the United States been involved in such terror, rioting and burning as erupted in Miami during the spring of '80. There were dozens of reasons given for what happened — the beating death of Arthur McDuffie; an unfair judicial system; lack of job opportunities; city politicians biased against blacks; and competition for service from social agencies that blacks believe favor the refugees flocking to the shores of southern Florida, especially from Cuba and Haiti.

MURRY H. SILL, THIRD PLACE NEWS PICTURE STORY, MIAMI HERALD

Photographer Murry Sill happened to be in a shopping center that was being looted by 500 or more people. Sixteen squad cars with 70 officers were trying to stop them. The policeman grappling with the looter forced him to the ground and arrested him. The officer with the gun aimed at another person (outside the frame) while his dog guaranteed that the man on the ground stayed there. The man shouldering his shotgun was a junk yard owner protecting his property. The Army Surplus store was photographed on Monday morning after the National Guard had been called in. On the first day of the burning, Sill made the aerial picture. Judges said that Sill's story "showed good judgment and good reaction to the physical challenges there."

On a sailboat named Eastern Star 103 Haitians arrived in Ft. Lauderdale. They claimed to have been at sea for 24 days from Haiti ... the immigration officer disputed their claim and suggested they'd come from Nassau in the Bahamas, about a four day trip. Some explained that they'd pooled their money to buy the Eastern Star to come to America "for a better life." They came penniless, carrying small satchels of clothing and had run out of food. When they arrived they were fingerprinted, photographed, placed with relatives or released on parole as illegal aliens. In Florida, this story is repeated daily.

WALTER STRICKLIN, SECOND PLACE NEWS PICTURE STORY, FLORIDA TIMES UNION/JACKSONVILLE JOURNAL

Incoming Cuban refugees already numbered 31,000 when President Jimmy Carter declared "No more boats." Walter Stricklin planned to do a story on a family leaving Cuba, arriving here and relocating. Instead he photographed the masses of people arriving at Key West. He said he felt happiness at witnessing family reunions but rage when Cuban prostitutes flaunted the fact that "this was their new country."

Hundred of Cubans "camped" in a sweltering hangar at Eglin Air Base and waited to be bused to Tamiami Park's processing center near Miami.

Stricklin wondered to himself if his own family had come to America with as much determination as the people he photographed.

A Border Patrol agent climbed between railroad cars carrying autos because illegal aliens sometimes hitch rides, even sitting in the new cars, as they are routed through Yuma, Ariz., north to Los Angeles.

TOM KASSER, SECOND PLACE RUNNER-UP, NEWSPAPER PHOTOGRAPHER OF THE YEAR, SAN BERNARDINO SUN

Beneath a California freeway overpass, one agent frisked an alien discovered hiding in the trunk of a car.

Since he is wearing an Angel's baseball cap, Photographer Tom Kasser said, "it may indicate the man behind the bushes has been north more than once before."

78

Members of the U.S. Border Patrol in California "are weary and cynical" said Tom Kasser. "They chase after illegal aliens as much as 12 hours a day . . . usually Mexicans . . . process them quickly and grant them voluntary departure back to Mexico. This means they can expect to catch the same person again in 24 hours. The job is an endless chase." "During the census the Border Patrol asked not to check residential areas since their actions might disrupt the final count. They were also banned from checking businesses and farms which depend heavily on illegal aliens as cheap labor. Car checks were halted because of pressure from Hispanic groups that charged the checks were discriminatory," said Kasser.

The story on this game of "hid and seek" was published as a special tabloid in the San Bernardino Sun.

Those picked up by the Border Patrol sleep in a detention cell until a bus comes to take them back to the border.

A Patrol trainee, Tom Cotter, napped after 12 hours of chase. Cotter, who is fluent in several languages, eventually resigned from his job with the Patrol.

79

When the day for the KKK rally arrived, all parties were expecting something eventful. Oceanside police quietly occupied several buildings adjoining the site. Back-up forces from the California Highway Patrol staged themselves a few blocks away. The KKK group was last to arrive, but came 30-strong, in riot gear, with hockey masks and shields and ball bats. They also had "bottles of soda pop, dogs and a few guns which they never drew." Meanwhile a large group gathered; hot, loud and partly drunk. When the KKK tried to leave, bottles and rocks began to fly. Both good and bad guys were targets. Dog handlers tried to attack people in the rock-throwing mob . . . one man was attacked by KKK-ers and beaten with ball bats. After the beating, police moved in, as a wedge. At one point, police shot a dog when one KKK handler tried to stand his ground. Many were hurt. No arrests were made. Photographer David Gatley said, "Covering the riot was as dangerous an occasion as I ever care to cover . . . yet, I'll be there again when the time comes . . . because the resulting photos remind people of the senselessness of such occasions. These pictures are the only hopeful products of an otherwise insane day."

DAVID T. GATLEY, LOS ANGELES TIMES

Near Damascus, Arkansas, a worker dropped the socket of a 3-lb. wrench. The tool fell 70 feet and ruptured a fuel tank in the silo of a Titan II intercontinental ballistic missile. Vapors escaped and immediately people in a five-mile radius were told to leave. Finally the mixture of fuel and oxygen blew the 750-ton concrete cover off the silo. One worker died; 21 others were hurt. Officials reported that no radiation leaked from the missile which was tipped with a multimegaton nuclear warhead. This incident and others which have occured in the past ten years reopened debate regarding the safety of Titan II missiles. Quoted in wire service reports and magazines the week of the blast, government officials assured citizens that the Titans are "a perfectly safe system to operate" and that the missiles are not obsolete. Fifty-four missiles are based in Arkansas, Arizona and Kansas.

MARK HUMPHREY, JACKSON SUN, JACKSON, TENNESSEE

PHIL SHEFFIELD, HONORABLE MENTION SPOT NEWS, THE TAMPA TRIBUNE

A Liberian freighter rammed into an abutment of the Sunshine Skyway Bridge and a 1,200-foot section fell into Tampa Bay carrying with it a bus-full of passengers, three cars and a pick-up truck. The bridge had been hit three times in four months. Only the driver of the pick-up truck survived. The driver of the car resting precariously at the edge of the broken span and his three passengers missed following the other vehicles by 14 inches.

An extortionist attached a letter to a large bomb and left it in the executive offices of Harvey's Resort Hotel near Lake Tahoe, Calif. Stories of the bomb's potential destructive force grew during two days of negotiations until bomb experts decided to detonate the device. The $3 million demanded in the extortionist's letter was never paid, but the blast did equal that much damage to the hotel and surrounding businesses. Photographer Ken Mirell said, "It was difficult to accept that Harvey Gross had no alternative but to risk the destruction of his entire enterprise. And I felt great apprehension during those final seconds because there was no protection from flying debris where I was shooting."

KEN MIRELL, TAHOE DAILY TRIBUNE

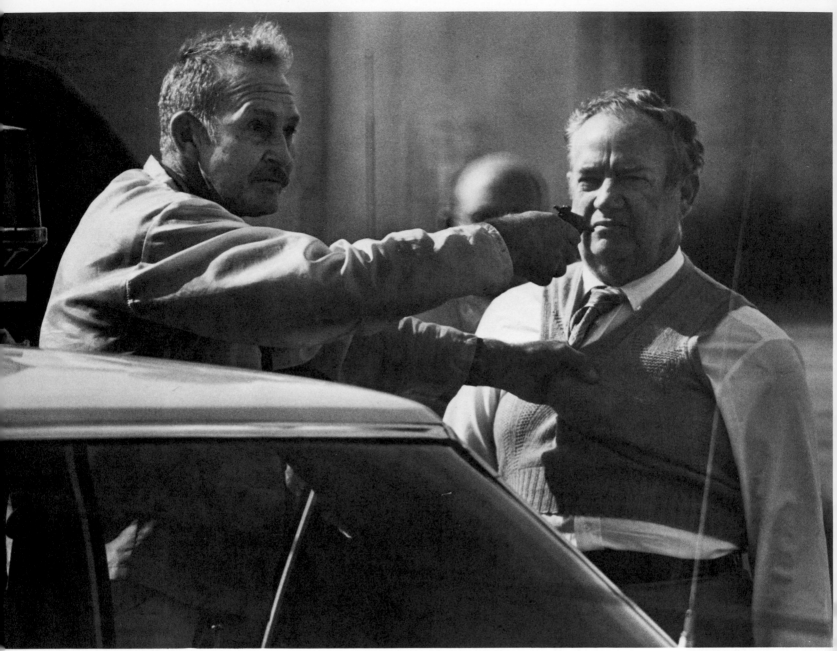

NEIL MCGAHEE, THE TAMPA TRIBUNE

Listening to his scanner on his way to work, Neil McGahee heard that a man was holding the St. Petersburg Fire Chief Zelmar C. Greenway hostage. The man was a former fireman, Hugh Chambliss. During a hearing that morning, Chambliss had been denied pension money. With a starter's pistol held to the face of the chief, Chambliss protested his dismissal and denial of money. Police surrounded the two and talked with Chambliss an hour before they persuaded him to release Greenway.

Death in the street. In Dallas, Texas, Gilberto Salazar, 21, was shot fatally in the head on the sidewalk near the Quarterback Lounge just minutes after he walked out the door. Patrons in the lounge heard two shots. Paramedics' attempts to revive Salazar were unsuccessful. Electrodes used in the attempt remained on the body when the picture was made.

TONY BERARDI, JR., FIRST PLACE EDITORIAL ILLUSTRATION, CHICAGO TRIBUNE

Judges complimented photographers who entered the editorial illustration category and said that this photograph on Lennon's sheet music and the glasses was especially creative. The title of Tony Berardi's illustration: "A Final Tribute."

Approximately 300 people gathered at the Lincoln Memorial in Washington, D.C. to honor John Lennon two days after he was murdered near his New York apartment. The group sang and chanted, burned candles and maintained a ten-minute period of silence during their vigil. Barbara Ries liked this photograph because to her, "it makes a very simple statement" about what she saw at that gathering.

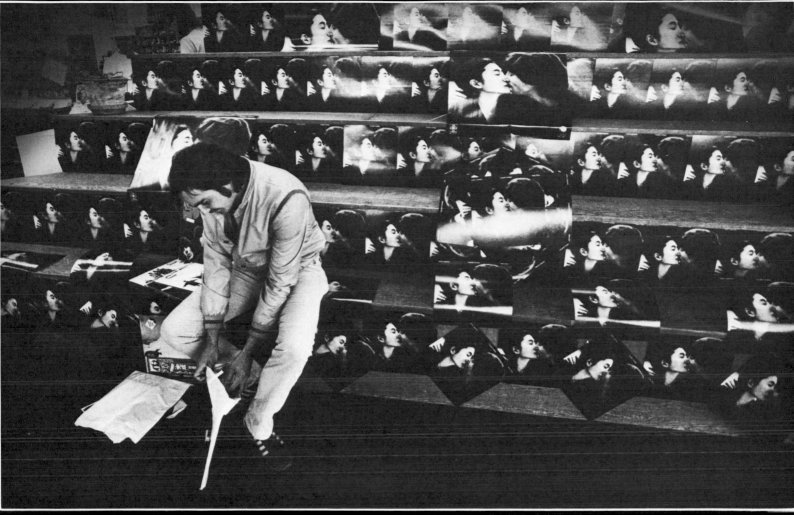

Record stores were swamped with people trying to buy Lennon's last album, "Double Fantasy." Brad Graverson photographed a customer sitting amidst a promotional display of that album.

The gates of the New York apartment house where John and Yoko Ono lived were covered with flowers, pictures and messages left there by hundreds of adoring fans.

Jim Colburn said the scene reminded him of something he'd seen at Lourdes, "the way people would leave crutches after a cure; very unusual, very European."

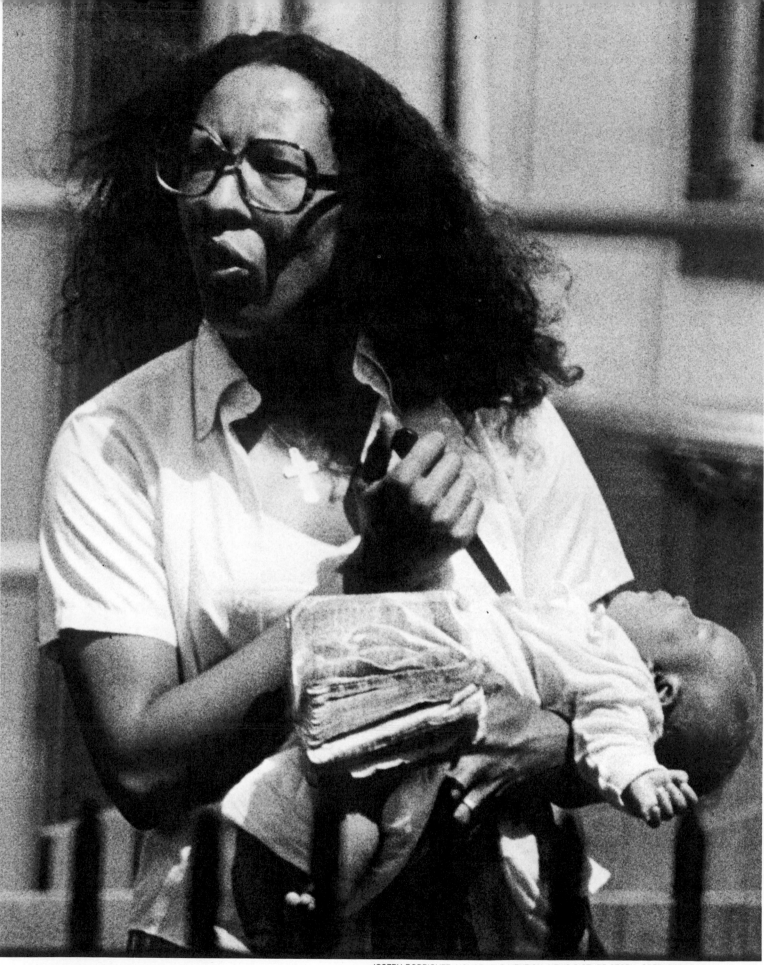

JOSEPH RODRIGUEZ, HONORABLE MENTION, NEWS PICTURE STORY, GREENSBORO NEWS CO., (N.C.)

Calling her baby a "demon and a vampire," clutching a Bible and knife to the baby's breast, Catherine Freeman protested a court order removing the baby from her custody. It was the fourth child to be taken from her by court order. A friend of hers wrestled the knife from her hand and police moved in. Freeman was handcuffed and the baby was carried away safely to the care of a paramedic.

TOM KASSER, SAN BERNARDINO SUN

RON HOSKINS, THE TAMPA TRIBUNE

The man in the storm drain survived; the little boy did not. While intoxicated, the man stepped into a 30-foot storm drain shaft. Residents heard his cries for help and alerted paramedics who pulled him from the hole. His unexpected fall gave him several broken bones. Efforts of six paramedics failed to revive the young victim of a swimming accident near Tampa.

Photographer Ron Hoskins was upset by the incident but believed the Tribune was correct in publishing the picture.

The 60 mph winds of Hurricane Allen were still blowing in Corpus Christi when Howard Castleberry photographed this sailboat owner checking for damage. The picture was five columns on the front page of the Dallas Morning News.

A pre-dawn phone call alerted Bert Fox to the collapse of a 70-year-old bridge linking southern Oregon with northern California. A train and its cargo fell into the Klamath River. Early morning sunlight caused steamy clouds to form and when railroad engineers began to survey the wreckage, Fox saw the picture he wanted.

Silhouetted against the afternoon sun, a fireman pitched smoldering hay after a fire at a hog farm near Hutchinson, Kan. The fire caused about $10,000 in damage but no hogs were injured or killed.

BERT FOX, MEDFORD (ORE) MAIL TRIBUNE

HOWARD CASTLEBERRY, THE DALLAS MORNING NEWS

PETE SOUZA, THE HUTCHINSON (KA) NEWS

On the coldest day of the year in Philadelphia, firemen fought a stubborn fire and were coated with ice. When Robert Dias saw fireman John Brett, he was startled by the thickness of the ice on his face, helmet and shoulders. Dias said that Brett's eyes told the story of bitter cold and fatigue as much as the ice that covered him. The picture was used three-columns on the front page with a story about how weather was affecting Philadelphians during one of its most severe snowstorms.

The driver of the station wagon lost control, the car skidded down an embankment and landed in the creek. The driver walked away shaken, but unhurt. Two tow-truck drivers struggled three hours to get the station wagon out of the creek.

ROBERT E. DIAS, THE BULLETIN, PHILADELPHIA

JOAN GARCIA, GANNETT ROCHESTER NEWSPAPER

96

MARK MORSON, ST. PAUL DISPATCH PIONEER

Mark Morson believes we often try too hard to make a picture when the one that tells the story is right in front of us. He made this one just after a fire (out of frame, left) on a bitterly cold day in Minnesota.

Dallas, Texas suffered 42 consecutive days of 100° heat in the summer of 1980. While ice was a hot commodity, Billy Copeland loaded and unloaded 50 lb. bags for an ice company.

MICHAEL S. WIRTZ, DALLAS TIMES HERALD

During Virginia's first major rainfall of 1980, Keith Howard was playing in the water on a Richmond city street. Lui Wong just happened to be driving by, looking for a weather feature.

Four persons were injured in an explosion triggered by heavy rains and a tree root. A gas leak formed after the root forced open a joint in the line. Relatives of those who lived in the house tried to salvage family belongings. The painting was apparently undamaged.

David Sommers stopped in downtown Saginaw on a December day to buy some film. He saw a little kid at a bus stop doing his best to stay warm and made four frames before the boy got on a bus and was gone. The picture was released over the UPI wire and used all over the country. In January the Saginaw News published the photo again in an attempt to discover who the boy was. His mother identified him. The headless bus-rider is Herbie White, age 10.

LUI K. WONG, RICHMOND NEWSPAPERS INC.

MIKE SMITH, DALLAS TIMES HERALD   DAVID A. SOMMERS, THE SAGINAW NEWS

Larry Price's pony-in-hurricane picture caused such a stir in Petronila, Texas, that a columnist in Corpus Christi, Roy Swann, took on the job of getting the facts in print. Because the picture was released over the AP wire, letters from all over the country poured in, complaining about the inhumane treatment of the pony. It turned out that the picture was made 12 miles from Petronila, and had the pony been inside either the trailer or shed near where he was tied, he probably would have been killed. Both trailer and shed were destroyed by the 90 mph winds of Hurricane Allen. The pony picture appeared in TIME and on page one of the Washington Post. (A fuller version of this story was published in the December, 1980 News Photographer magazine.)

A tornado struck Kalamazoo, Mich. and took five lives. Three were killed in the collapse of this seven-story department store, which, in this picture, looks like a child's battered dollhouse. The car is on top of a three-story parking ramp next to the store.

The cow in the net swung close enough to bump Greg Greer off the top of the truck from which he was taking this picture. The helicopter pilot, Larry Quick, airlifted 26 head of Charlais to solid ground after they were trapped by a Mt. St. Helens mudflow. Quick accepted one cow as payment for the day's work.

In spite of his dive through the dirt under the head of an irritated bull, this cowboy escaped with only cuts and bruises. The Brahman bull-riding event in any rodeo is probably the most dangerous for the cowboy; this one bit the dust at the Orange Show Rodeo in San Bernardino. Photographer Tom Kasser described bull riders as "almost always young and slightly crazy." The cowboys gamble on the chance that they can get away faster than a bull can shake his head from side to side.

GREG GREER, FREELANCE, COLUMBIA, MISSOURI

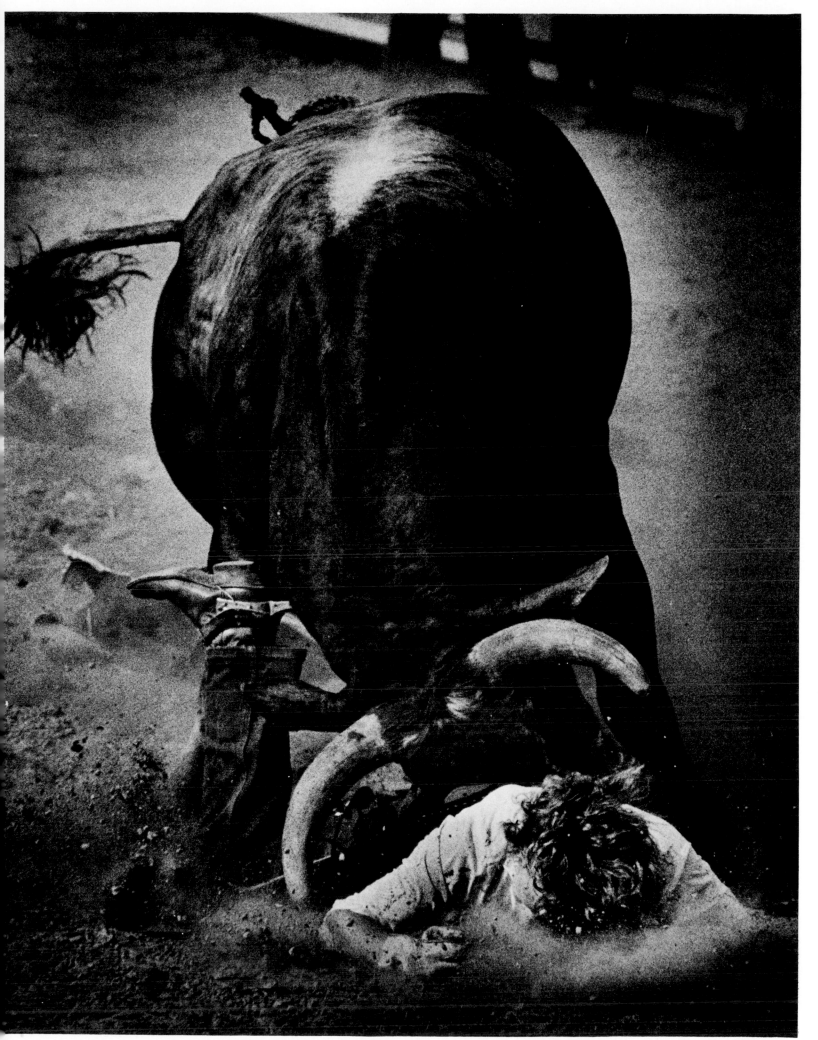

TOM KASSER, FIRST PLACE SPORTS ACTION, SAN BERNARDINO SUN

Faces

Nothing is as compelling to a photographer as the human face or animals that innocently mimic humans. We are fascinated with ourselves.

Studying the following pictures will be like walking through a hall of mirrors. We are moved by what we love and respect as well as what we pity and fear. We are overwhelmed by our strength and our fragility. We wonder if eyes are truly windows to the soul. We would not be surprised to learn that soul and brain operate independently of each other.

People live longer these days, but why have whiskers on old men become symbolic of character?

Faces of the famous and the infamous, rich and poor, young and old, melt into a pool of human images indistinguishable from one another until a photographer isolates one or two individuals and tells us a story in a portrait.

To cover events, one must understand the situation, be in the right position at the right moment and follow the action to tell the story.

To cover character, one must understand, or at least accept the person who is his subject. One must approach from a proper vantage point and have the sensitivity to respond to people with a degree of intimacy.

The challenge of photographers in the portrait/personality and features category is to show us more than what we see with our eyes.

Would Neil Leifer's winning portrait (far right) be a better picture if Coach Paul (Bear) Bryant's hand were in the frame and he was holding a piece of chalk? TIME editors thought so. The frame was used for the September 29th cover and included both hand and chalk. Sixty years with winning football teams made Bear Bryant a man of "supercoach" stature. TIME labeled him "the dominant figure in college football" as leader of Alabama's Crimson Tide.

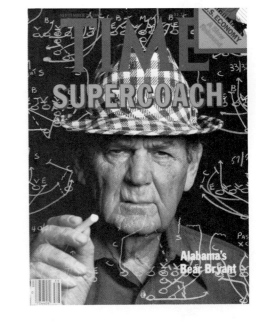

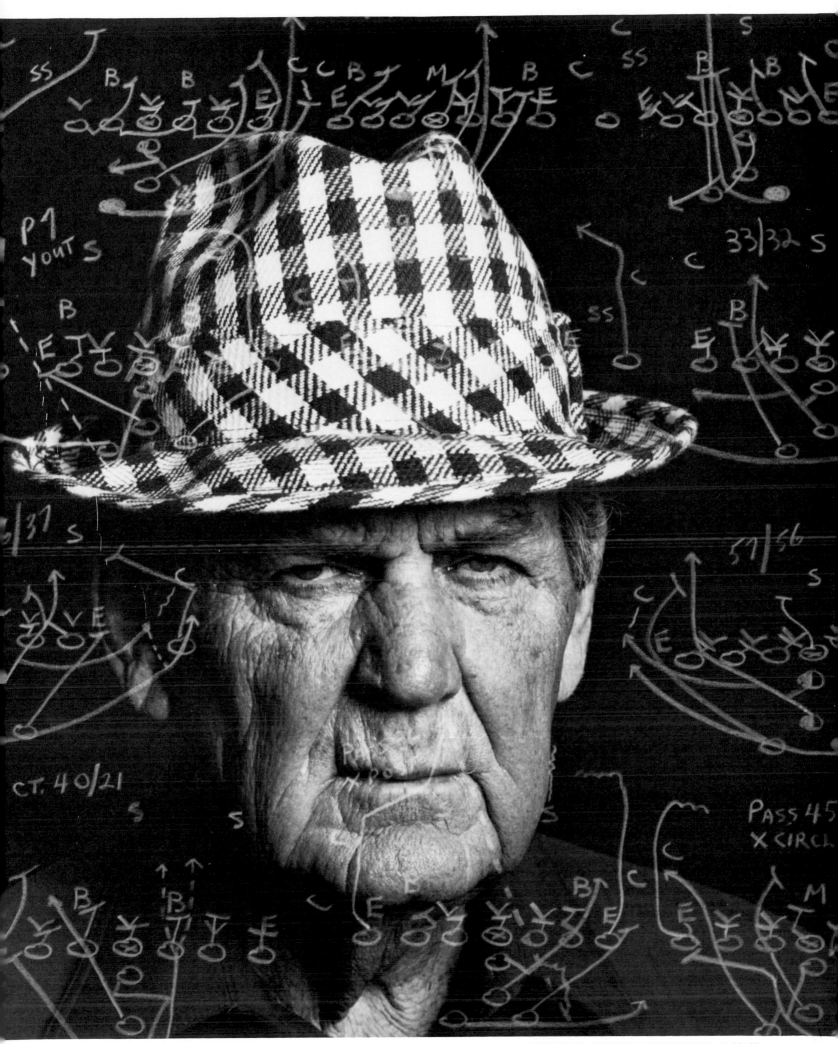

NEIL LEIFER, FIRST PLACE MAGAZINE PORTRAIT/PERSONALITY, FOR TIME MAGAZINE (ORIGINAL IN COLOR)

Former star quarterback, Joe Namath played the role of "Little Abner" in a community theatre in San Bernardino.

Mickey Rooney appeared in the Broadway bash, "Sugar Babies," at age 59, bouncing through the burlesque with the merriment for which he has been known all his acting career. This picture was a LIFE magazine cover.

The famous Betty Davis eyes popped as she yelled at photographers during a press conference, "No nostril shots." Photographs were allowed only from the front; still and television photographers were not to shoot at the same time, and the word and picture people were divided during the conference.

Below, a Chinese sailor, Lu Ming, smiled at his first glimpse of America. He was aboard the first ship from China to dock at the Port of New Orleans in 40 years.

Above is the haunting face of an elderly Chinese woman whose portrait is used on the cover of Eve Arnold's book "In China" and was included in LIFE's article on changes in China.

Dressed in her finest winter clothes, a Catholic Chinese woman stood in her family courtyard, beaming at her grandchild. The portrait was made for GEO magazine.

The title of this illustration establishes the point of the picture, "Foreign students — caught between languages." Brian Smith's model for this illustration is Ann Wen-Chang, graduate student from Taiwan, herself a photojournalist. She supplied some Chinese characters and a few words of English, in chalk on a classroom blackboard. Smith photographed the blackboard and then made a studio portrait. The double-exposure was used with a story about the language problems that foreign students face.

On this spread and on page 105, we note what we hope has not become another cliche in technique, figures drawn on a blackboard to symbolize some part of a story, over or around the subject of the photograph. The judges picked two such photos as winners this year.

BRIAN SMITH, COLUMBIAN MISSOURIAN, HONORABLE MENTION EDITORIAL ILLUSTRATION

ミセス ティンカー
たぶち ちょうこ

LARRY ATHERTON, THE JACKSON SUN

KERRY COUGHLIN, SEATTLE POST-INTELLIGENCER

Choko Tabuchi, seven-years-old, writes the name of her teacher in Japanese. The private school Choko attends organized afternoon sessions to help the new, young Japanese students learn English. This picture was used in the LIVING section of the Jackson (Tenn.) Sun with a story about the influx of Japanese in Tennessee and their difficulties with a new language.

Benjamin Ng is a tired dragon dancer who twirled through the streets of the international district in Seattle in a birthday celebration for the Republic of China, Taiwan.

BILL KESLER, ST. LOUIS POST-DISPATCH

C.W. GRIFFIN, MILITARY PHOTOGRAPHER OF THE YEAR, U.S. NAVY

Richard Nixon was to leave his Park Avenue townhouse for the Shah's funeral. Gathering newsmen served as a signal to passersby that "something was happening." Among the curious were these four women.

A Navy photographer visiting Piccadilly Circus recorded the displeasure one spectator registered at the appearance of a group of people dressed in "New Wave" style. The glance askance was cast from a passing bus.

The title of this picture? "Inflationary Headache." During President Carter's administration, Arthur Burns served as Director of the Federal Reserve Board.

113

KIT C. KING, SUN NEWSPAPERS, OMAHA, NEB.

While on assignment to photograph elementary school children touring a farm, Kit King saw the puppet hanging from the window of a car. He thought the picture was funny, included it in his portfolio and has been surprised more than once by other people's response to it. The picture of the hanging Ernie puppet and the winning feature picture of two inmates passing time with a game of hearts force viewers to ponder the fine line between what is funny and what is sad. With a steel wall between their cells at Menard prison (Chester, Ill.) huddling in the corners and reaching through the bars is the only way inmates can play a game of cards. There is an added note of humor; the title of the book on the floor is "Lovejoy's Career and Vocational School Guide."

JERRY LOWER, FIRST PLACE FEATURE PICTURE, NEWSPAPER DIVISION, THE SOUTHERN ILLINOISAN, CARBONDALE, ILL.

WILLIAM W. THOMPSON III, SSGT., USAF, NORTON AFB, CALIF.

116

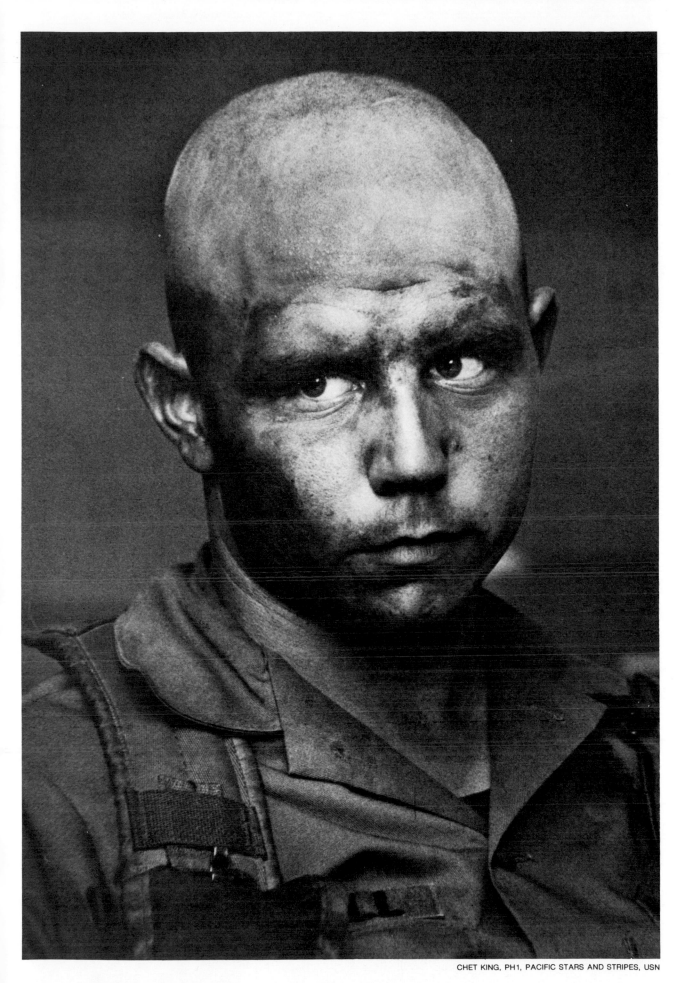

William Thompson explained that a lot of patience and a little bleach (ferricyanide diluted with fixer) helped him duplicate what he saw while photographing this Airman in lizard-colored face paint. Bounce flash in a Quonset hut is reflected off the head of a young Army man who was learning to be a military leader at a school in Camp Casey, South Korea.

BOTH PHOTOS: MARTHA LEONARD, FREELANCE, CHICAGO, ILL.

Jane Byrne and her husband/press secretary were so incensed that Martha Leonard released this picture to "Us" magazine, that Leonard was demoted from her job as Mayor's Official Photographer. Once word got around that she lost her job because of the picture, AP picked up the photo and it ran in many large and small newspapers in the U.S. The picture was made backstage at the Chicago Fest when the mayor went to greet John Belushi and Dan Ackroyd. Leonard asked the mayor and her daughter Kathy to put on the hats and glasses that the Blues Brothers were wearing, and they did. The picture is frame # 36, and first ran in the February, 1980 "Us" magazine.

After Jane Byrne was elected mayor of Chicago, she was regularly swamped by autograph seekers. The picture of her in the midst of the crowd on the city's Navy pier, was used as promotional material for the 1980 Chicago Fest. Leonard believes this picture typifies the dilemma Mayor Byrne faced each time she appeared in public during the first few months in office.

Nine young dancers await their turn at a Church of England garden party at London's Hurlingham Club. The original photograph is in color and the judges were intrigued by the fact that eight of the nine girls are wearing headbands of different shades of lilac. The girl leaning on her arm in the lower left corner of the picture wears a blue-green head band. All the dancers are dressed in white. Judges also felt that the fact that the girls are pressing their heads against the glass, apparently unaware of the photographer, gives the viewer a feeling of anticipation shared among the dancers. The subtle tones and overall mood of the photograph remain intact, even in black and white.

PATRICK WARD FOR GEO MAGAZINE, FIRST PLACE FEATURE PICTURE, (ORIGINAL IN COLOR)

ROBBIE BEDELL, THE TAMPA TRIBUNE

Sam Stokes and his family pick tangerines in the groves of Pasco and Hernando counties in Florida. The patriarch leads his large crew from crop to crop, winter and summer. Stokes has harvested fruit and vegetables since he was six. His portrait was published as part of a picture page on citrus picking and the Stokes family.

Viewers can appreciate a picture more when they know the story behind it. That is true of this portrait of a woman who was twice a refugee. The photographer discovered through a reporter who spoke Spanish, that this woman left Lebanon for Cuba to escape World War II, then left Cuba with her daughter to seek a new life in America.

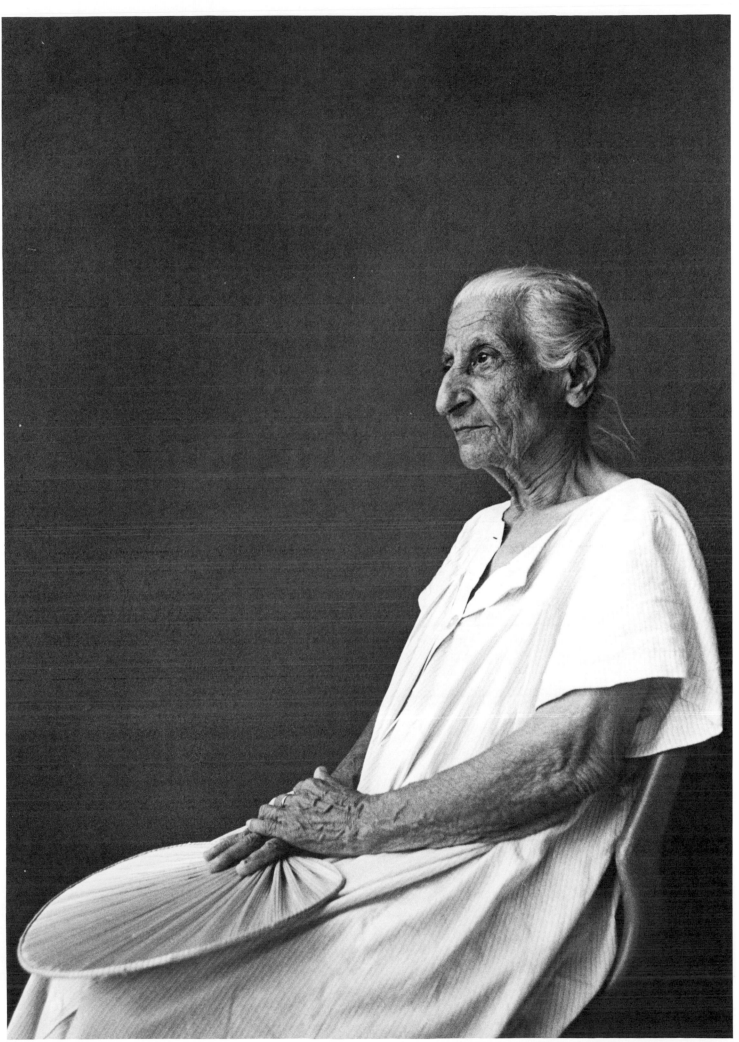

While Peter Ensenberger studied photojournalism at Arizona State University, he photographed a chaplin at the Newman Center, Father Greg. The picture was used as an illustration with a story on campus religious life.

An effort by Dave Williams to capture "quiet dignity" was successful in the photo of the woman in the chador. Changing her name from Donna to Ra'shualaamu Beruni, she adopted the dress and life style of the Muslim faith. Her new name means, "mysterious, powerful, peaceful one."

DAVE WILLIAMS, WICHITA EAGLE-BEACON

Old Joe was sitting on the edge of his wheelbarrow. Close by was his dog, Budweiser. His face parallels the stories he tells passersby ... about being a mule skinner and his life as a pioneer; about his brother fighting in World War I. He is a celebrity in Skagit Valley, but no one, including himself, says how old Joe really is.

Minnie Garrett, 101, was a resident of Serenity Haven Nursing Home in Garland, Texas. For most of her life she was a farm wife and a seamstress. For her three years at the nursing home she was active in church services. Minnie's portrait was used on a picture page about men and women over 100 years-old. Minnie Garrett died a few months after this photograph was made.

M.H. Mason is his name but he is known as Old Bluegill. He is a 77 year-old Cherokee ... proud and defiant. "I'm just an old, wild one. You can't tame me. It's been tried." Old Bluegill lives outdoors on the bank of a canal in Canal Point, Florida, and spends his days fishing for bass, and of course, bluegill.

JIMI LOTT, SKAGIT VALLEY HERALD & YAKIMA HERALD-REPUBLIC

RANDY ELI GROTHE, THE DALLAS MORNING NEWS

JOHN COLEY, PALM BEACH POST

More than 100 people died in Kansas City as a result of the heatwave of 1980. Ninety-three-year-old George Ousley suffered but was one of the survivors.

Arnett Hillhouse played the role of St. Nick for the first time in his 67 years. He said he is eager for next season, but in the meantime he'll shave and clean-up and will hope to be mistaken for Kojak.

Judges said they were drawn into this portrait of W. J. Cleveland because of the technical excellence of the photograph. Photographer Bill Wax said that the 57 year-old face reflects the ravages of time and alcohol.

BILL WAX, SECOND PLACE PORTRAIT/PERSONALITY,
GAINESVILLE SUN

Greg Smith was to photograph Mr. and Mrs. Robert Miller of Bartlesville, Oklahoma, for an article honoring their 60th wedding anniversary. The couple was unable to come to the newspaper's studio for the portrait, but Smith welcomed the opportunity to visit their home. He hoped to find something there that would suggest their long life together. Since Mrs. Miller was unable to stand, he asked Mr. Miller to pose near her chair. Smith chose to keep the picture of Christ in the background. He made the portrait with a 24mm lens and bounce flash and was disappointed to "find the picture buried in the Sunday women's section."

Because of a story to be done on the 100th anniversary of the Salvation Army, Talis Bergmanis received an assignment to photograph the local historian, Mary Morrissey and the highest ranking lady in the Rochester area, Brigadier Lottie Brunner. Bergmanis set up his lights in the living room of the house they share. When he told them he was ready to start shooting, they spontaneously held hands. For Bergmanis, it was "a delightful element, unanticipated, in what was otherwise a controlled situation." The women have been companions for 35 years. Bergmanis was working for Gannett Rochester Newspapers in New York when he made this picture.

KAREN BORCHERS, DAYTON JOURNAL HERALD

Photographer Karen Borchers and writer Janet Filips produced a story titled, "It's a honey of a hobby," for the Dayton Journal Herald. Beekeepers Wesley and Bernadine Owen had ordered a few pounds of bees (with two queens) from a Sears & Roebuck farm catalogue in 1945. Wesley Owen got interested in bee keeping while in the Army and was quoted in the story saying, "I just like bees; I just like to fool with 'em, you know what I mean? . . . They are smarter than we are; they make honey and we can't. We can go to the moon, but we can't make honey."

For robbing the hives, Owen and his wife dress in white, "the bee's favorite color — from veiled safari hats to coveralls, to long gloves." Owen explained that the best time to rob the hives is on a hot, humid day when the bees are "not mean at all." When it is cloudy and rainy is not the time to "fool with 'em." The Owens lend their hives to farmers whose fields need pollinating. He said that people can't do without bees. When they see a swarm, they should get hold of a beekeeper. And above all, "Don't kill them. That's one thing they shouldn't do is kill the bees."

TALIS BERGMANIS, GANNETT ROCHESTER NEWSPAPERS

George and Mary Robinson own and operate a nudist camp near Syracuse, N.Y. They posed for Talis Bergmanis in their living room, in their usual attire. The statue at right was a Christmas present to them from their daughter.

But that is just the end of this story. It began 12 years ago. Bergmanis worked for the Rochester-Democrat & Chronicle at the time. Since there were several nudist camps in the area, the editors accepted the photographer's suggestion that a story with pictures was in order. Bergmanis visited Empire Haven twice and yes, doffed his clothes.

(George and Mary assured him that it would be easy and that he would get used to it. It wasn't. He didn't. He said he felt uneasy the entire time.)

He made pictures and wrote the story which climbed the editorial ladder until someone decided it was inappropriate for use in the Sunday magazine. Three years later editors of a city magazine thought the story was a wonderful idea. Bergmanis went back to George and said he was there for more photos. The story was scheduled for publication in August, but the magazine folded in July. Then six years later, an editor who had

liked the story the first time said, "Let's try it again." Bergmanis went back to George saying he needed more photos. George was friendly as always but said, "Some people around here are wondering if you really work for a newspaper. You've been shooting 12 years and nothing's been published yet." Then finally, in August of 1980, the Rochester Times-Union published a page and a half. It is understandable why Bergmanis heaves a deep sigh when anyone asks him to tell the story behind this picture.

DAVID A. PICKEL, THE DAILY PRESS, INC. NEWPORT NEWS, VA

David Pickel was out searching for a feature picture when he saw Tony Smith performing alone with a frisbee. Smith was practicing his skills with the silicone-coated plastic disk on the campus of Hampton Institute in Hampton, Va. Pickel encouraged him to do his leaping, twisting and stretching routine for the camera. The result was a multiple-picture package for Pickle and an entertaining feature for Daily Press readers.

Brian Smith created a visual illusion when he took this picture of Preston Chancellor standing near a wall. What appears at first to be shadows cast by persons outside the frame are parts of a mural painted on the Julius Rosenwald Center wall in New Orleans.

BRIAN SMITH, FREELANCE, CINCINNATI, OHIO

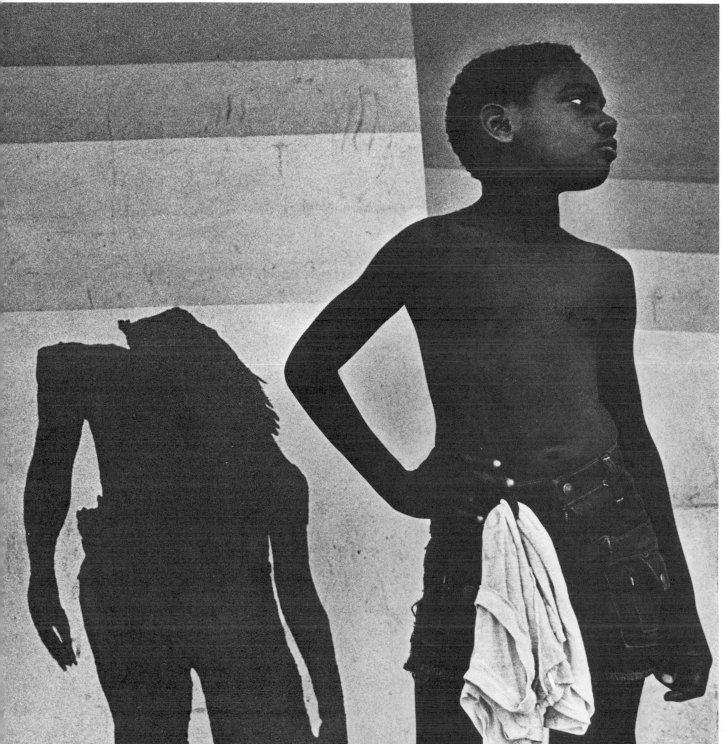

RAYMOND K. GEHMAN, THE MISSOULIAN, MISSOULA, MT

JOY WOLF, SAN JOSE MERCURY-NEWS, CA

Two buffalo-head nickles hang from the neckpiece of Pablo Bellon, a young Flathead Indian living in Bozeman, Mont. Bellon was dressed in costume for his part in a powwow among tribes of Northwestern Indians who have gathered annually for 80 years. Raymond Gehman and writer Richard Eggert teamed up to produce a two-page photo story on tribal gatherings and ancient Indian songs.

A fragile elegance describes the effect that strong back-light gives this photograph. Silvana Granados is a member of Lupe, a children's Mexican dance company. The group performs its own interpretations of folkloric dances throughout Santa Clara county, Calif.

Too hot and no space to float a boat. Photographer Skip Peterson found 10-month old Zerrick Columbe of Dayton, Ohio, being cooled by a helpful grandmother. This kid-in-tub picture has a different twist in that the tub is a kettle and it's being filled with jars and bottles of water.

Too big for the kitchen sink. Doug Milner discovered that sometimes the best pictures are ones taken just for fun. His nephew, Damian, was discovered playing in the dirt in a new Easter suit. He was escorted to the sink and given a thorough swabbing. The light and Damian's delighted expression made a picture out of what Doug figured to be just a snapshot.

Too young to play ball with the big kids. Dana Kidwell, 3-years-old, held his bandaged finger and watched his brother's first day of practice with the peewee league in Tiffin, Ohio.

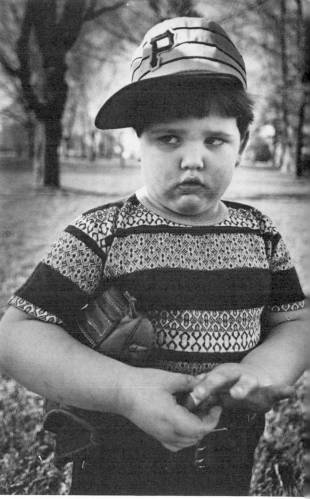

LANCE WYNN, THE ADVERTISER-TRIBUNE, TIFFIN, OH

DOUG MILNER, DENTON RECORD CHRONICLE, DENTON, TEXAS

SKIP PETERSON, DAYTON DAILY NEWS, DAYTON, OH

139

LEN LAHMAN, FREELANCE

Truck-beds are ready-made sets for the drama of child's play. The message on the bumper reads, "Hi guy, my name is Timmie and this is my little kooden rat truckie." That, and the two flat tires, plus the

varied and unrelated expressions on the children's faces makes this photo a study in incongruity.

Mennonite families retain their religious and cultural values even

on the vast, high plateaus of Central Mexico. There, a horse and buggy is still a luxury. The case of cola bottles gives this picture a time reference that nothing else in the photo provides.

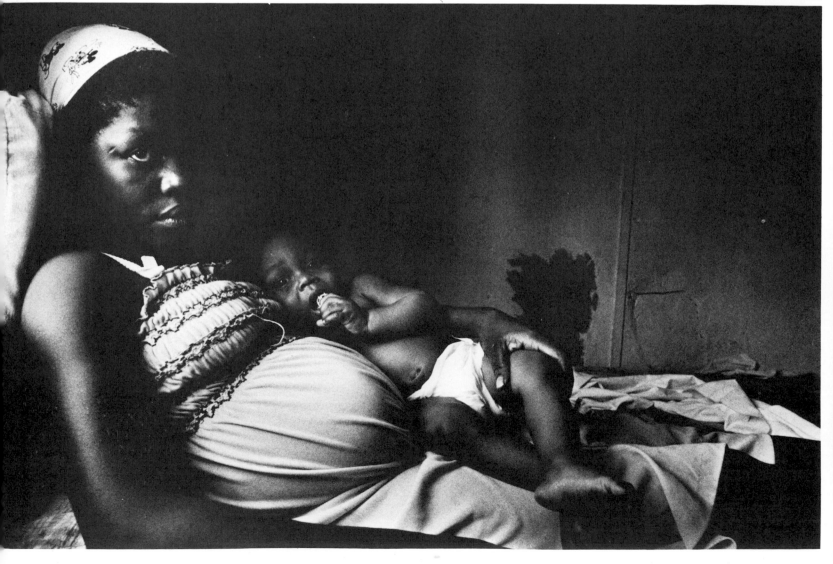

Groups of refugees were being moved about the city of Miami to 1), provide space for family groups and 2), clear the camp at the Orange Bowl to accommodate the upcoming football season. Keith Graham was sent to a run-down hotel late one evening to get pictures of families who had been moved. Hurrying in hopes of using natural light, he used a service elevator to the third floor and photographed two groups before he found Evelio Acosta and his nephews. He knew when he met them that they would make the picture he was looking for. The editors liked the picture well-enough to send a reporter to talk to the Acostas; the picture was held for the story, then was printed the next day on page one.

The portrait of Rose Mane Davelse and her son, Luck, was used in a page and a half of pictures with a story that photographer Neil McGahee produced about misery in Miami's Liberty City ghettos. He found a family of 24 living in one 5-room house. Only one member of the 24 had a job at the time. They were friendly but skeptical because they thought the photographer might be an agent of Duvalier's secret police force. Discrimination against the hundreds of refugees in southern Florida sometimes makes living conditions and employment opportunities worse than the ones from which they fled, especially for Haitians. McGahee explained that the Haitians are a confused and frightened people. They fear the immigration officials who will send them back to Haiti, American blacks who consider them unwelcome competition for jobs in Florida and the dreaded "Ton Ton Macoute" (secret police) they believe to be operating in America.

A Haitian child watched from a distance as missionaries conducted a service in a crowded school room in Obis. This picture was not used in the series about the missionaries to Haiti, but was published later in a special section on refugees. In the time lapse the child, who the photographer said is a girl, became identified as a "boy watching a group of visiting Americans touring the little fishing village of Obis."

C.J. WALKER, PALM BEACH POST-TIMES

Richard Gordon, 94, met Ruth Harris, 88, and after a two-year courtship, they were married at the Episcopal Church Home in Louisville, Ky. Photographer Jim Wright produced both story and photos for a feature that included this picture of the couple returning to their room after the reception. Picture editor Lisa Roberts did the layout of Wright's work, but neither of them knew if the story would be printed that day. It turned out that the Times had an open half page.

On her way down a side street in Tecate, Mexico, where she was on assignment to cover the running of the bulls, Melanie Kaestner found this barber shop. She stood in the doorway and asked to take some pictures and the barber was so cooperative that he would turn the customer in the chair to face the camera, and pose proudly with a broad smile. So she left. Later she stopped in again. This time the barber tired of posing and after about 20 minutes, the man in the chair pulled a whiskey bottle from under the sheet and the barber paused with "a wonderful look of anticipation ... a very simple moment in time ..." said Kaestner.

JIM WRIGHT, THIRD PLACE FEATURE, COURIER-JOURNAL & LOUISVILLE TIMES

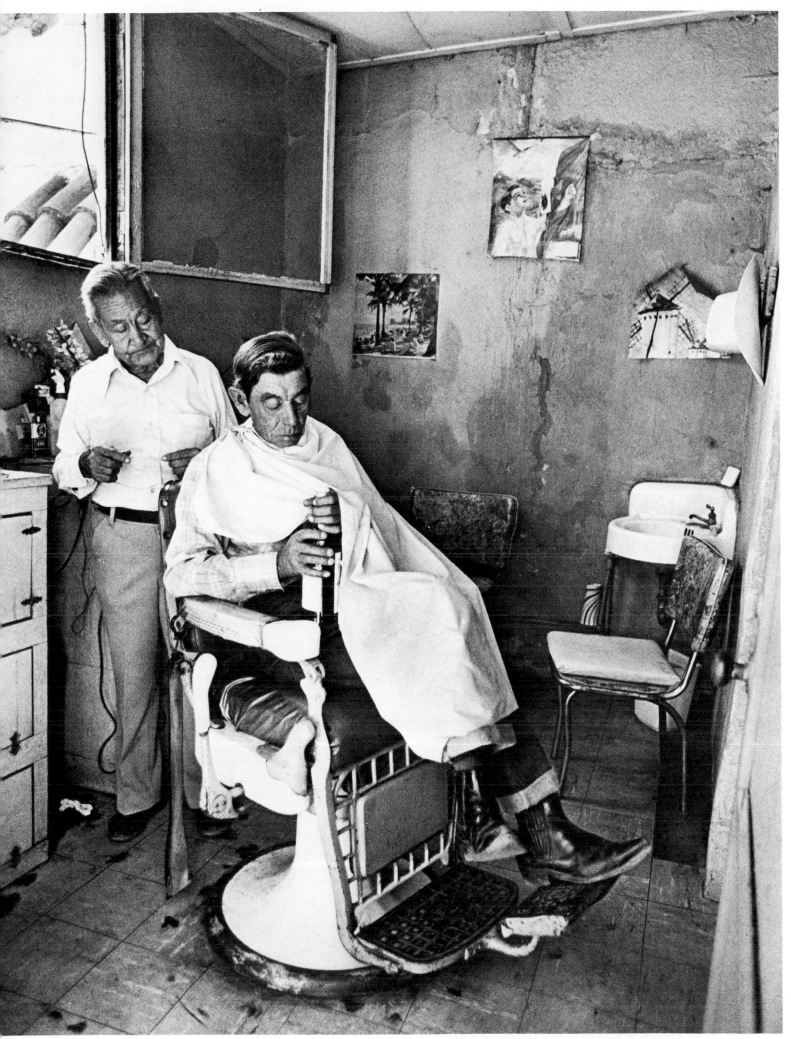

The pictures of animals which seem to be appreciated most by readers, are those which capitalize on the human characteristics of the animals. (pages 28-29 and 200-201) Sometimes it is a human that mimics the animal, (right, top). Editors publish birth announcements for zoo animals more eagerly than they handle such announcements for humans. Such was true of the picture above that covered the protective care of a new-borne sea lion at Sea Life Park in Honolulu. Baby sea lions are called "pups" and this one is Kaiopua's first.

JOHN L. RUSSELL, TRAVERSE CITY RECORD-EAGLE,
TRAVERSE CITY, MICHIGAN

*John Russell recorded a bear-to-
bear meeting of actor J. Drew
Pickard and a real bear at the zoo.
The bear in the cage was nervous
as long as Pickard kept the head of
the costume on. When he
removed it, the real bear appeared
to lose interest. Publication of the
picture was a plug for a school
play, "The Cave Dwellers."*

*It would be anyone's guess as to
whether Frosty, the polar bear at
the Philadelphia zoo, registers
feelings of boredom, contentment
or fatigue while straddling a log in
his new outdoor quarters. Looking
at this picture, people have asked
if Frosty is really just a bear rug
draped over a log. Viewers do
react to Frosty's body language
saying, "wow; that's just how I feel
sometimes."*

BOB SACHA, THE PHILADELPHIA INQUIRER,
PENNSYLVANIA

147

World Understanding

Warren's Guardian Angel

Bryce Flynn, Providence (R.I.)
Journal-Bulletin

Medical science has extended the lifespan of many terminally ill people. A debate now rages between those who believe human life should be extended at all costs, and those who feel the quality of life to be the primary consideration. The story of Warren Grunberg, a severely retarded teenager whose mother Carol has almost single-handedly kept him alive since his birth, is a study in extremes. Warren's afflictions are extreme: they have left him at age 14 with the physical and mental abilities of an infant. But no less extreme is the devotion of his mother to making his life as comfortable — and as long — as possible. It is easy to accuse Carol Grunberg of selfishness; it is difficult to meet her and not feel humbled by her courage. It is easy to cite reasons why the boy would be better off dead; it is difficult to look into his mother's face and even consider those reasons. It is easy to see that Warren will never become a "productive member of society;" it is difficult to meet the family's many friends without appreciating how much tenderness he has inspired in others. The story of these two private lives contains the quintessence of all that both sides of the public debate are about. An outsider must face the horror of what is Warren's life, but must also acknowledge the way that horror is tempered by a mother's simple love. It makes us look at the other side of the arguments and forces us to face the truism that any doctrinaire answer must be at least half wrong.

Bryce Flynn was photographing a pediatric care operation in a Providence hospital when he met Carol Grunberg and her son Warren. A nurse described the angel painted on the ceiling of Warren's bedroom at home and Flynn decided he had to make that photograph. After several visits to the Grunberg home, Flynn convinced Carol that she could receive support from and be an inspiration to many other people who were learning to deal with problems like her's. At the time she was having difficulties with the Rhode Island state health insurance agency that was attempting to force Warren into a state institution by withdrawing financial support for his care. She had been divorced and was also involved in a suit against the doctors that delivered Warren. Flynn worked carefully with Carol's lawyers to assure that no phrases or information could be used against her in a court of law, yet, in the text, answers to questions readers would have were clearly satisfied. Warren's early life was precarious but Carol refused institutional care. As he reached puberty, his condition worsened with frequent seizures and respiratory infections. When Flynn's story was finished, it was published in the Providence Sunday Journal Magazine as a cover and six pages with no advertising. Although the text and captions are sympathetic to Carol's accommodation of her son's needs, the point of his usefulness in inspiring such motherly devotion provokes serious questions about the struggles to preserve such a life as Warren's.

Warren's diapers are checked and changed near the television set in his recreation room where he spends most of his time at home. Carol Grunberg believes the music and excitement are enjoyable to him. He responds little but when his mother is in the room he keeps his eyes on her.

For a stroll in the sunshine, Warren rests in an oversized buggy that his mother pushes through the neighborhood where they live. "I know my son will never play baseball, or go out on a date, or get married. I even know he probably won't be around much longer, though I really can't face it. But I get more joy from the little things he does than anyone else could possibly get from their child's first step or first word. Because that's all expected from a healthy child. Everything Warren does is a victory."

Warren's bed is a sick-bed with padded rails and oxygen bottles standing guard near the Mickey Mouse telephone. Over his bed is a guardian angel. The painting bears a strong resemblance to his mother.

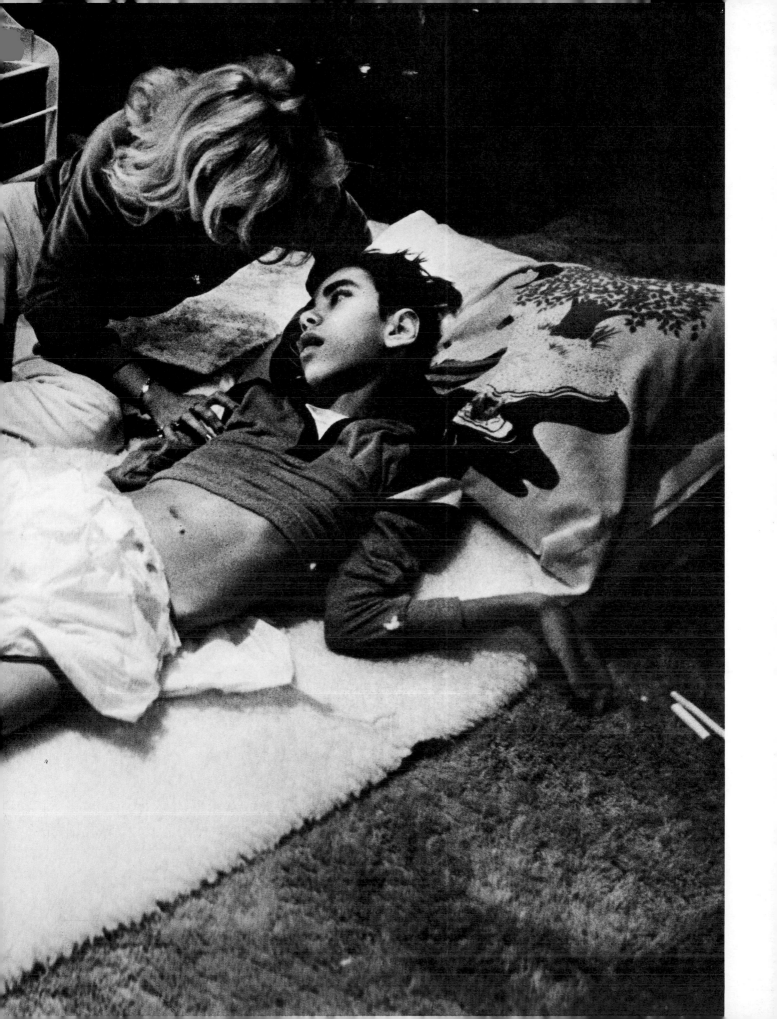

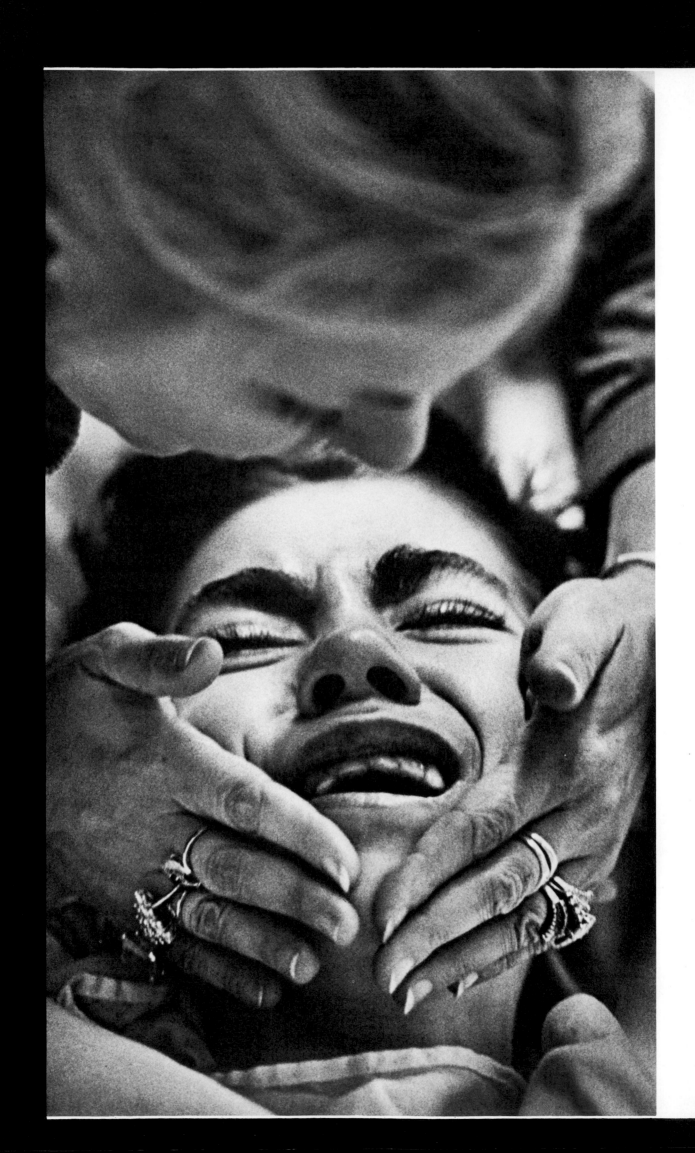

World Understanding
Special Recognition

Anna and Flander Hamlin
A Lifetime Shared

David C. Turnley, Detroit Free Press

One cold November day in 1978 when I was driving to work, I passed a farm and noticed an old man and woman out near the barn cutting some huge logs. The sight of this couple performing such heavy work made me curious. As I got out of my car, I said that I was interested in the way they were cutting wood and did they mind if I just watched them work for awhile.

They didn't say much. In fact, it wasn't until I mentioned I was from Indiana that they seemed to let down their guard a little. Indiana is their home state, too. So, we talked about the weather and about my work at the local newspaper and about the wood they were cutting to heat their home that winter.

When I asked if I could take a picture of them together, they became suddenly shy again, not understanding why anyone would want to take their picture. Finally, just to be polite, they took a position in front of the barn, and as I stood peering at them through my camera, the old man's arm reached around the woman's shoulders in a protective gesture. That was my first photograph of Anna and Flander Hamlin.

When I returned later to show them the picture, they invited me in for a cup of coffee. In the three years since, I have often been back.

Anna Hamlin is 79 and Flander, her husband since 1924, is 81. They live forty minutes west of Detroit, Mich., on a fifty-acre farm that they have worked for the last 26 years.

I was 22 when I first met them, and marriage had always seemed to me a little like cutting off your arm and giving it to someone. Yet here were two people who had been married for 56 remarkably uneventful years and still seemed to enjoy being together as much as ever. It became important to me to understand why.

Anna and Flander Hamlin are a man and a woman of strength, grace and pride whose life is less endowed with material things than many, but fuller than many, too. What makes life valuable to them is the simple things that are part of each day: working together to put food on their table, caring for their family and friends, and having faith in their religion and in each other.

The self-sufficiency which they have by working together on their farm stands in contrast to the stereotype of the elderly as helpless and dependent.

While people like Anna and Flander Hamlin do not live to set examples, there is a nobility in what they are and what they do that transcends the generations.

For Anna and Flander Hamlin,
laughter and love go hand in hand.
Between and after their chores,
much of their time is spent
together like this.

*As their dog Lady looks on, Anna
lets Flander sample some of her
pumpkin pie. They call this area
under a large tree next to their
house "the office," and so long as
it stays warm they can be found
there nearly every evening.*

While out repairing the fence one day in early spring, Anna and Flander shared a private and special moment.

Together Anna and Flander climb
up the ladder to the loft to stack
bales of hay that weigh between 25
and 35 lbs. I have seen them move
a couple of hundred bales in a day.

Anna unhitches a wagon-load of hay
that is then fed to the few horses
they board or, it is sold to horse
farmers in the area for a little extra
income.

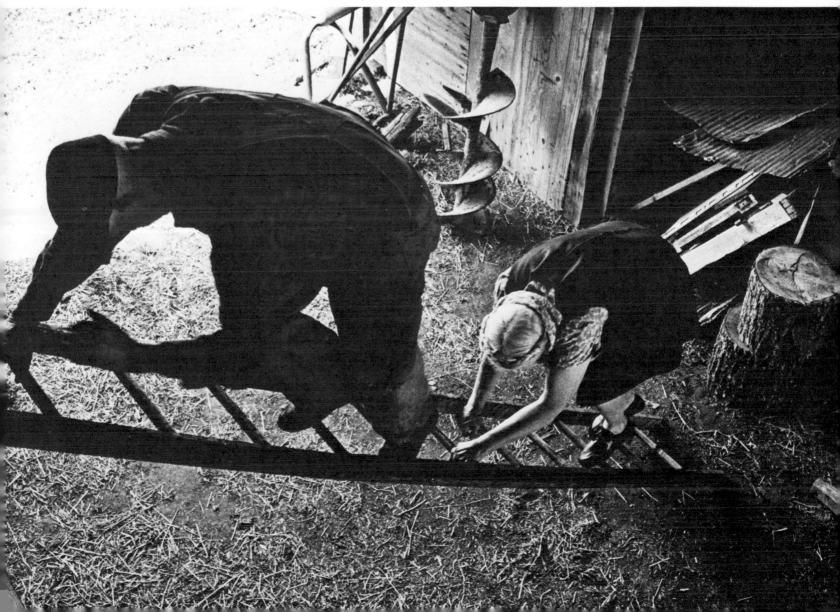

Anna gathers a few tomatoes to boil so that Flander can peel off the skins. They put up enough to last through the winter and into the following growing season.

Winter evenings are often spent playing dominoes at the kitchen table.

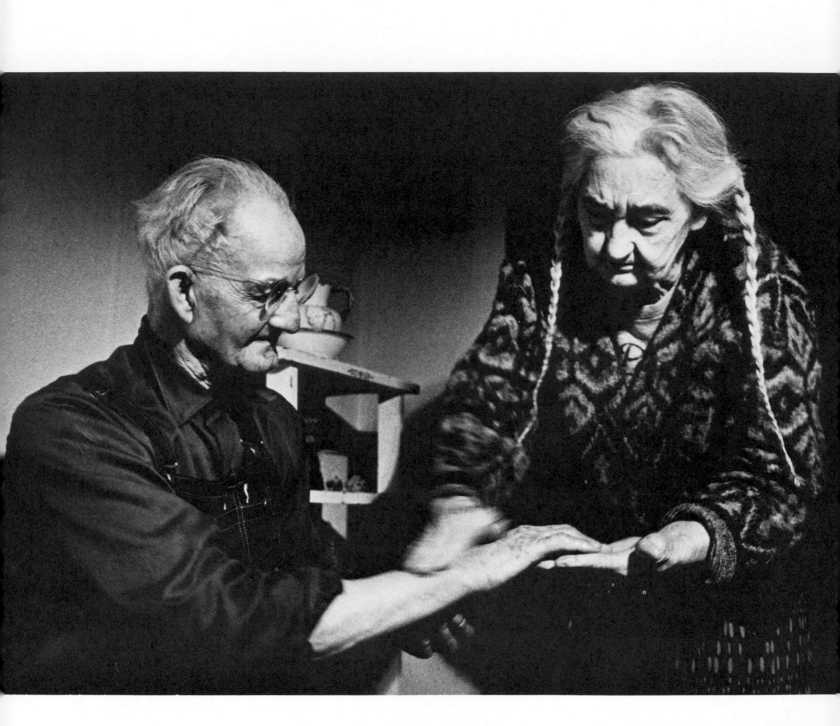

Flander has trouble from time to time with a skin rash, psoriasis. Before going to bed, Anna rubs a prescribed ointment on Flander's arms and hands to soothe the irritation.

Flander helps Anna with a hard-to-reach zipper as they get ready for Wednesday prayer meeting.

The church is an important part of
Anna's and Flander's life. It is also
the focal point of their social
activity.

Each night before going to bed,
they read the Bible together, then
kneel and pray.

ALL PHOTOS PAGES 157-169, DAVID C. TURNLEY, DETROIT FREE PRESS WORLD UNDERSTANDING SPECIAL RECOGNITION

Anna and Flander raise vegetables in their large garden — beans, corn, potatoes, onions and tomatoes.

On a warm, spring day, even the laundry shares the togetherness evident in the Hamlin household.

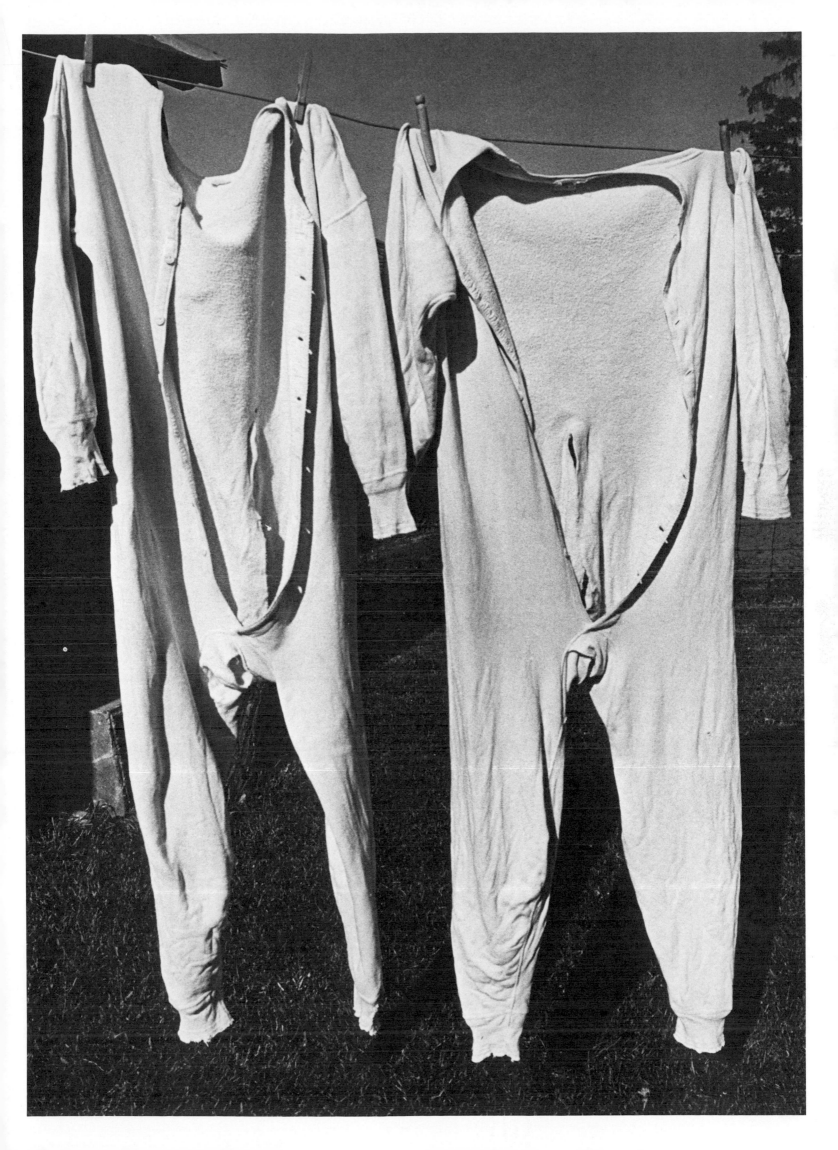

Feature Stories

There are seven stories in the section that follows, selected for their variety of approach ... from simple to complex subjects.

They are humanistic stories that reveal details about those lives that grab the imaginations of curious people.

These stories prove that no subject is trite, when, because of the effort of the photographer, we understand it better. The trick is finding an unusual approach to a much-used topic.

Newspapers are becoming more sophisticated in subject matter, treatment and display of full page stories or multiple picture packages. More photographers are being responsible for producing an entire piece — pictures, story, captions, headlines and layout.

Given time and opportunity to complete such feature stories, photographers must supply the most important ingredient for success; that is, a good *idea.*

Some picture stories can be three or fewer pictures and require only a few hours work; others need several pictures and may require months to complete. Still, the best ones depend on the *quality of the idea.*

The photographer who has *ideas for stories,* with the energy and skill to pursue them, is the one who will get the better job and keep it.

PATRICIA BECK, DETROIT FREE PRESS

Sister Alma Reilly is a Detroit Tiger fan and has spent 73 years as a nun, 50 of them teaching in parochial schools throughout Michigan. She celebrated her 100th birthday with her friends at the Immaculate Heart of Mary Motherhouse infirmary, her home for the past 22 years. Except for failing vision and hearing, Sister Alma is in good health. She was baptized Emma Reilly in Paddy McMahon's Saloon where Holy Redeemer parish met before building its first church. Since she is an avid Tiger fan, members of the team have sent her autographed baseballs and paper weights. Much of her time at the Motherhouse is spent in prayer, or visiting with other nuns, or listening to Tiger baseball on the radio in her room.

"Money is no problem," insisted Mother Teresa. "The Lord sends it. We do his work. He provides the means."

And about praying, "You have to do your work as if everything depends on you, then leave the rest to God."

Photographer Mary Ellen Mark and writer Harriet Heyman produced a twelve page story for LIFE (July, 1980) about "Teresa of the Slums — a saintly nun who embraces India's poor." Mother Teresa, 70, was awarded the Nobel Peace Prize for her Missions of Charity, 158 houses all over the world that care for those most desperately in need. Mary Ellen Mark spent a month documenting the work of Mother Teresa and kept a diary that is quoted throughout the LIFE article.
"In this extreme of suffering, pus, blood, vomit, urine, screams, sad and vacant faces — the sisters never stop working; they are gentle and kind. Each time I ask something, the sister tells me, 'It is God's work; don't you see? You should put down your camera and do some work.' Quite honestly, I don't think I could."

Wearing the white sari that denotes her allegiance to India's poor, Mother Teresa feeds a sick man.

MARY ELLEN MARK, FIRST PLACE FEATURE PICTURE STORY, MAGAZINE FOR LIFE (ALL PHOTOS: PAGES 172-179)

Nirmal Hriday is the hospice for the dying that Mother Teresa created on the grounds of a temple to the goddess Kali, the Hindu "dark mother" of death and destruction. When the poor arrive at the hospice, filthy and eaten by vermin and disease, they are washed, their hair is cut and their wounds dressed. The sisters and brothers help them get better or at least try to give them a measure of peace before death.

"Most people's gentle acceptance of death is amazing," noted Mary Ellen Mark." 'They are all people completely alone,' a nun told me. 'Very sick, poor and with no one. The men die much faster than the women. The women take a long time to die.' "

"I watched this man die," reported Mark, "struggling for breath, sunken cheeks, huge terrified eyes, restless, in pain. He dies. His eyes do not shut."

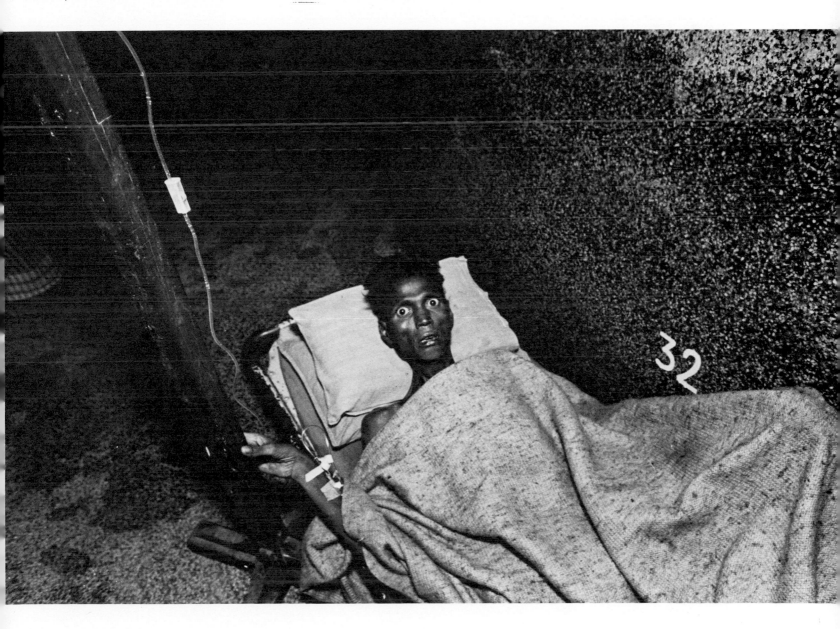

In the washing room at Nirmal Hriday, nuns gather up rags and sheets to boil in vats. The white door leads to the morgue where the body of the man will be delivered.

In her diary, Mary Ellen Mark continued, "In the women's room nuns mop and bathe the women — excrement everywhere . . . several new patients.

. . . their legs drawn up like fetuses. Some can't control their bodily functions. That's often the most sad, because they realize their loss of control and are ashamed.

"The women are fed lots of food, the sisters mop up again, then medicine, injections, clean beds, then lunch of fish, vegetables and rice.

". . . The nuns work so hard, oblivious to the most terrible sights and smells . . .

". . . Some of the women have an automatic begging gesture. They are old, senile; so many years they have raised their hands to beg, they cannot stop."

The nuns go home at 6:30 to eat, have a bit of free time before night prayers and retire at 10. They rise at 4:30 every morning to pray, do housework, wash out one of their two saris, attend mass and eat a breakfast of bread and tea — and begin work again.

At Prem Dan (Gift of Love) which is another part of the Calcutta mission, there is treatment for the insane. "The nuns play games with the patients, always laugh, never punish," noted Mark.

ALL PHOTOS: MARY ELLEN MARK (PAGES 172-179)

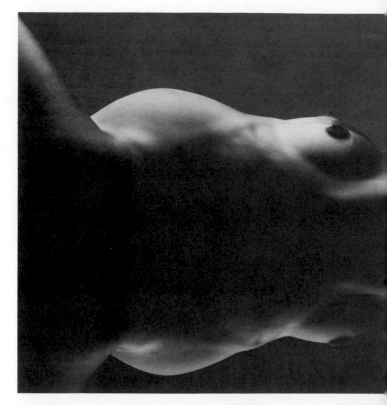

Judges comments on Gary Parker's essay, "Miracle of Life" were complimentary in this manner ... "the simplicity of design, the beautiful lighting and powerful composition made this series especially memorable. It was an idea that worked."

Jamie Glen Parker was born the day before Christmas. The series on his wife's pregnancy was "a purely personal document" Parker said. He set up a makeshift studio with a 2400 watt-second light source, and used Plexiglas to create a mirror reflection.

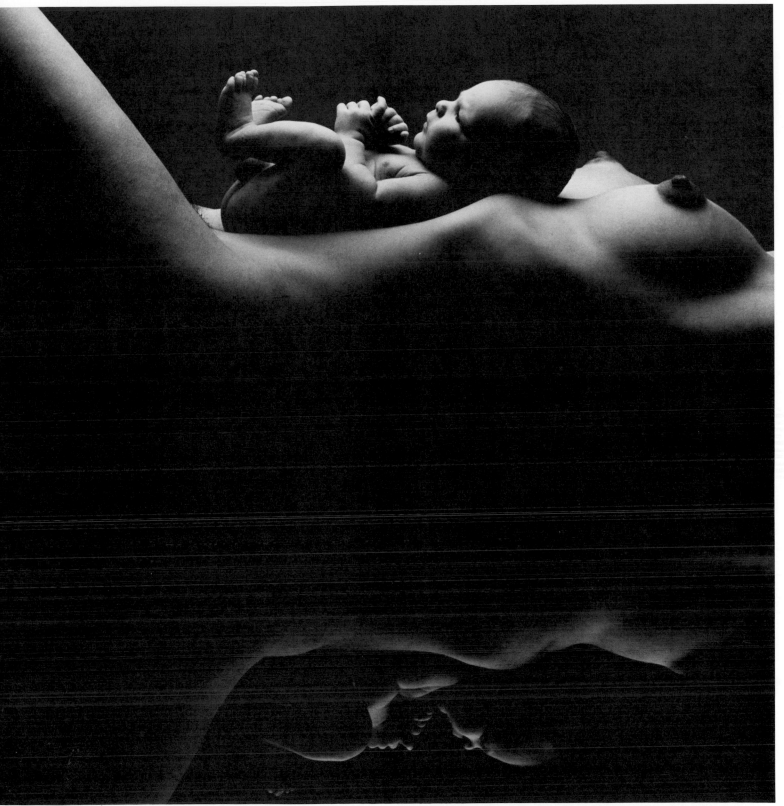

Julie Parker was shy and uneasy about being photographed nude, but overcame those feelings after she and her husband were convinced that the pictures would, "commemorate the birth of their son, forever." Together they felt that the essay was "something that should be shared."

Parker originally had reservations about showing the series, but once he and Julie shared the photographs with friends and discovered the favorable reaction the pictures received, he decided to enter the essay in competition.

JAY B. MATHER, FIRST PLACE FEATURE PICTURE STORY, COURIER-JOURNAL & LOUISVILLE TIMES

A group of about 40 Mennonite families moved
to Casey County, Kentucky when land became
scarce in the famed Amish region of Pennsylvania.
They brought with them a sincere desire to
remain out of the spotlight and were therefore
uncomfortable with the team who did the story.
Photographer Jay Mather and writer Byron
Crawford spent a day in the community,
discussing pictures and story ideas, eating with the
families and watching them work. A tentative
resolution was reached; one suggested by one of
the ministers, Brother Oberholtzer ... the rules
were to be, no posing of pictures, no pictures
inside homes and no pictures during church
services.

With the rules established as to how the story
would be done, Jay Mather hoped he would not
miss too much.

One old-time Mennonite teaches a new member
how to operate horse-drawn equipment used in
the annual wheat harvest.

"If we need livestock or produce hauled to
market, we will hire someone with a truck,"
Brother Oberholtzer explained.

"For regular farm work, we try to stay to the horses. It's not that we think tractors or electricity are evil within themselves. But there's always a temptation to go out further — endless horizons to fill the mind. We believe our life should be a life of service to God."

The picture of the group standing around the yard of an old house they use as a church, talking, was not one he had predicted. It was after services and the group was still divided, male from female, young from old. With the younger boys watching him, curious and fascinated by the camera . . . and the women in the background on the back porch, the situation was most revealing about the Mennonite sect. The Gentle Residents of Casey County was published on the 4th of July. The story emphasized freedom that all Americans enjoy; religion, speech, congregation, as well as freedom in mode of work, manner of dress and rights to privacy.

Oberholtzer and his wife, Mabel have 17 children, eight of them at home. Their neighbor, Phares Shirk has 11; most of the families in the Casey County settlement are large.

The personality of each boy gleams through the required conventional dress of his forefathers. And during church services, hats are hung aside.

PETE SOUZA, HUTCHINSON (KAN) NEWS

Esther Dellenbaugh, 90, was missing cattle from her 160-acre farm near Norwich, Kan. The sheriff and county attorney were unable to help her because, they said, the cattle were not identified in anyway. So, she said, she "had to let it rest." She offered a $25 reward for their return. "That ought to give a little incentive, hadn't it?" she said.

Photographer Pete Souza said the Hutchinson News planned to publish the story after his first visit to the farm, but Mrs. Dellenbaugh called and had second thoughts about use of the photos. Souza agreed to show her contact sheets; something he'd not done with a subject before. She flipped through them and said he had missed the best picture; one of her feeding the cows by hand. "Well, I just about died when she told me that, and proceeded to take a long trek to the pasture." That trek gave him his key picture.

Fourteen-year-old Dan Gage of Columbia, Mo., was equally at home behind a football mask or a handbuilt window frame of one of the miniature houses he builds as a money-making hobby. Dick Van Halsema Jr. produced a picture page on Gage for the Columbia Missourian. The story was part of a portfolio with which Van Halsema won the title, College Photographer of the Year.

DICK VAN HALSEMA JR. COLUMBIA MISSOURIAN

Officer Bud Harrington, ex-Los Angeles Ram guard, is a member of the San Jose, Calif. bicycle patrol. Knee pants, crew socks and "skid lid" helmets draw whistles from coworkers and startled looks from citizens, especially when they are issued citations for traffic violations. Officers patrol a 20-square-block area in the heart of the city. They say they can respond to calls faster because they can cut through alleys, ride down sidewalks and travel the wrong direction on one-way streets. Harrington and the team keep a close watch on people from astride a bicycle ... that may mean following a prostitute or arresting a man for public drunkeness.

The story was part of the portfolio that earned George Wedding the title, Newspaper Photographer of the Year.

Color Magic

The effectiveness of color photography in newspapers and magazines is often dependent on the quality of reproduction. Many photographers believe that use of color for color's sake is an expensive mistake.

Advertising experts can show how easily readers are seduced by color. Some photographers develop a sixth sense called "chrome vision," especially when they are expected to bring back color in addition to black and white. However, experienced photojournalists have learned to communicate with the subtlety of color.

One master of the craft is Cary Wolinsky, runner-up for title of Magazine Photographer of the Year. Wolinsky considers both pictures on page 194, "gifts . . . north light pictures . . . lucky shots that you just know are good the instant they are seen." (After just one frame, the rooster flew and the horse withdrew, but Wolinsky had the picture.)

Color photography can show us why something is beautiful; (vinegar bottles on page 207) - color suggests mood, time or temperature; (camels and oasis, pages 10-11 in the opening section of this book) - color helps us understand nature such as in the markings on the skins of animals; (Bengals, bison and buddies; pages 200-201). Who could say such pictures would be better in black and white?

One-third of the color pictures that follow were made for use in newspapers. In each, color enhances the message. In some, such as the fashion photograph of the red and green hats and dresses, (page 196) color IS the message.

The result of Eve Arnold's 40,000 mile trip across China is a large collection of photographs documenting change in that country. LIFE magazine published 12 pages of photos in October, 1980, from Arnold's book, "In China."

She shows us a surprising study of how China's leap into this century affects its people. The photographs affirm strength, simplicity and beauty of the country and its people. Here are two portraits of Chinese women participating in the changes now occuring. The woman with the wrench is a 20-year-old oil worker who earns $80 per month and lives in a dormitory with other laborers at the Victory oil fields. (Each dollar buys five times what it would in the U.S.) The woman in pink is a member of the Golden River White Horse Company in Inner Mongolia. She is training her horse to lie still so that in case of battle, she may shoot over him.

BOTH PHOTOS: EVE ARNOLD FOR LIFE MAGAZINE, THIRD PLACE NEWS OR DOCUMENTARY PICTURE STORY, MAGAZINE DIVISION

Cary Wolinsky photographed Idalie Penn in St. John, the U. S. Virgin Islands. In her national park job, she portrays herself, an effort by the government to show visitors that life there is comfortable and the citizens contented. It was a slow day at the park. Idalie was making lunch, and in the fine light, Wolinsky made several good pictures in a half hour. Blessed again with that bright north light, Wolinsky grabbed the scene below with a small automatic camera. The horse and rooster appeared for only a moment; long enough for one frame. Barn, chains and animals are near St. Agatha, Maine.

Jerry Jacka photographed Hopi Indiana carver, Jerry LaCapa in Walpi, Arizona, north of Winslow. (far right) LaCapa carves kachina dolls resembling dancers in Hopi religious ceremonies. Photography is usually prohibited in Hopi villages. Years of visits to the villages helped Jacka gain the trust exhibited by LaCapa; even so, the carver took one very long morning deciding to allow this picture to be made.
Jacka photographed LaCapa for Arizona Highways; daylight film, available light for one second at f/16.

CARY WOLINSKY, RUNNER-UP, MAGAZINE PHOTOGRAPHER OF THE YEAR FOR NATIONAL GEOGRAPHIC (BOTH PHOTOS ON THIS PAGE)

JERRY JACKA FOR ARIZONA HIGHWAYS MAGAZINE

The same picture but a different frame was reproduced 10 x 14 as a Style front for the Dallas Times Herald. Judges complimented Mel McIntire for his dramatic use of color and composition. Although composition is still impressive in black and white, it is red and green that excite. (Dress designer Michaele Vollbracht called these his "Belmont racing dresses.")

MEL MCINTIRE, THIRD PLACE FASHION, ILLUSTRATION, DALLAS TIMES HERALD

FREDRIC STEIN, SECOND PLACE FASION ILLUSTRATION, CHICAGO SUN-TIMES

Fredric Stein photographed the country gents on a horse farm near Suburban Chicago for the Sun-Times. The magazine caption described the double-brested suits as "thoroughbred classics" but did not mention the horse in the background. Judges said Stein "brought a little extra" to fashion photography in this photo.

After photographing a parade of models to determine which girl had the face to compliment the headdress, David Walters made this picture with a medium format camera. It was used on the cover of TROPIC magazine in a September fashion issue for the Miami Herald. Male judges were fascinated with the exotic quality of the picture. The female judge said, "It doesn't do a thing for me, but her face is pretty ... it makes a good cover."

DAVID WALTERS, FIRST PLACE FASHION ILLUSTRATION, MIAMI HERALD

TED SPIEGEL, HONORABLE MENTION, MAGAZINE FEATURE PICTURE STORY, FOR NATIONAL GEOGRAPHIC MAGAZINE

Twenty-nine photos appeared in National Geographic with an article about water as "our most precious resource." This Navajo medicine man sand-painted his prayer for rain. During the summer of 1980, about all that was left to do in some parts of the U.S. was pray for a break from the drought.

Viewers are struck with the "painted" quality of the picture (top) of West Germany's Fortuna-Gasdorf coal mine. West Germany's reclamation techniques set examples for the rest of the coal producing world, including the U.S. LIFE published both photos on this page with long stories about coal and gold.

At right, a gold miner grins over three nuggets worth at least $10,000. In a year, 25,000 men dug $50 million in gold from Serra Palada, a mountain in Brazil. At the time, gold was valued at $600 per ounce.

NATHAN BENN, FIRST PLACE SCIENCE AND NATURAL HISTORY, FOR NATIONAL GEOGRAPHIC

A temple of sculptured stone designed to look like one built in Asia years ago, provides a night-time shelter for two Bengal tigers, Natasha and Nikolai. The temple and tigers are in Miami's Metrozoo and the picture was used in a book titled, "Zoos Without Cages" ... produced by National Geographic Society especially for children.

Two bison enduring a March blizzard reminded one judge of a painting by an artist from the Old West. The picture is part of Jim Brandenburg's winning portfolio in the magazine division.

A frog playing pal to a winking turtle is the kind of humorous juxtaposition every photographer hopes to find eventually. Bianca Lavies calls this shot a lucky one, "one of those never repeatable moments." Because the camera has caught animals in gestures close to human, the level of our enjoyment increases.

Bamboo, the giant grass. The peoples of Asia use bamboo in hundreds of ways. Slatted swords for the ancient Japanese sport of kendo are made of bamboo. Hong Kong's scaffold riggers, operating like an exclusive craft union, tie strips of split bamboo to building facades. Some are known to have withstood typhoons when steel framework has crumpled.

Carrying pigs in a radial bamboo poke demonstrates the strength-to-weight ratio characteristic of the remarkable grass. In comparison, the tiny basket for a "five raison picnic" shows how precisely bamboo can be split and woven.

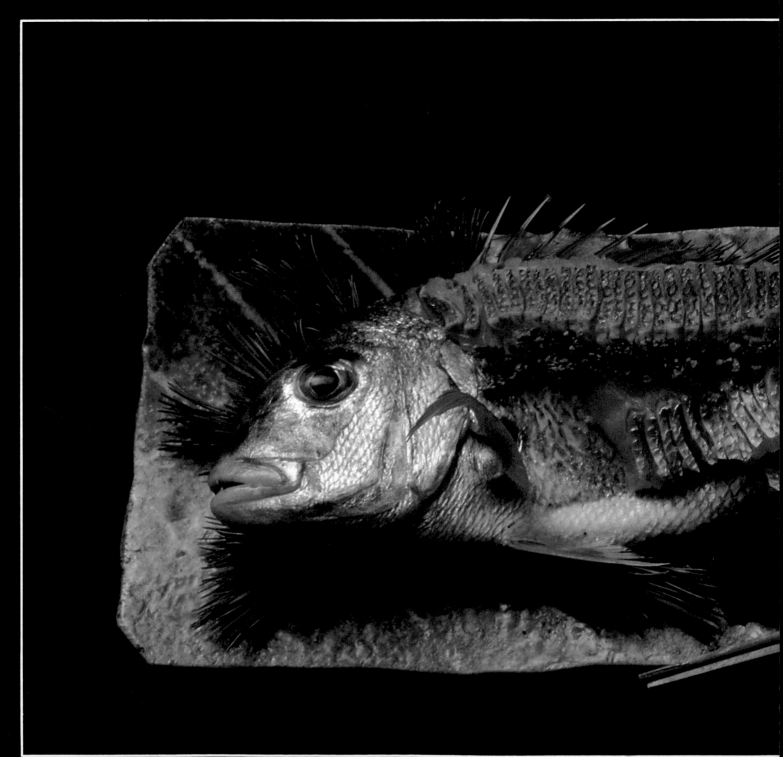

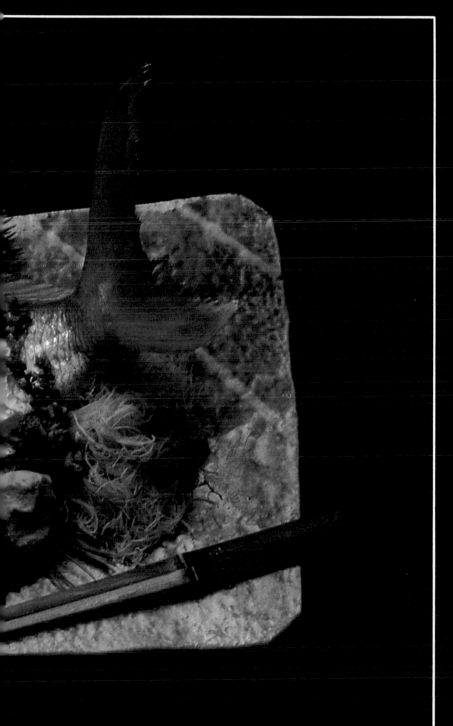

Shikibocho, the fish-slicing ceremony. Masatoshi Ikama bows, displays his wood-handled knife and steel chopsticks, and with a prescribed number of strokes carves the fish. Ikama is not a cook. His role is to cut up the fish in ceremonial style. After his performance, diners adjourn to another room where portions of the just-sliced fish are served with a meal.

Japanese food and the artistic manner in which it is prepared and served have become fashionable in the United States. Sea bream, sliced and reassembled is an example of the variety of raw fish called sashimi.

German photographer, Reinhart Wolf, has a speciality of photographing architecture, but with writer, Lionel Tiger, was excited by the idea of a story on Japanese food. "Art You Can Eat" was a 23-page feature in the March issue of GEO magazine.

Color food illustrations appear more frequently these days in newspapers and are usually elaborate productions for magazines. Many decisions about details and a lot of time for preparation go into producing them. The same photographer who spent his morning chasing a fire truck might spend his afternoon chasing spaghetti under a flood light. Versatility is one key to success in photojournalism.

Judges said that popcorn, which is not a colorful subject, did make a colorful picture because of the skill of the photographer. The photograph was titled as popcorn is labeled, "the nutritionally beneficial snack."

GARY PARKER, THIRD PLACE FOOD ILLUSTRATION, FLORIDA TIMES-UNION

Red pots, a cloud of steam and the sheen on the pasta combine as the inviting elements in the photograph. It is a before-and-after study in a single frame. Both color and texture entice the viewer, precisely what food illustrations are supposed to do.

Bottles of aged vinegars are subjects for a good illustration that capitalizes on atmosphere and subtle color for its effectiveness.

ROY SCULLY, SECOND PLACE FOOD ILLUSTRATION, SEATTLE TIMES

EDWARD R. NOBLE, THIRD PLACE SPORTS FEATURE, THE OAKLAND PRESS, PONTIAC, MICHIGAN

Liquid lightning ... the ebb and flow of a Sunday afternoon football game ... a photographer's attempt to relate motion using a slow shutter speed.

The resulting blur suggests contact and gives the picture a "painted" effect in this effort to get away from the standard football action shot.

Because it was felt that the colors were too subtle for News-Journal reproduction, the photo below was not published. Film was 400 ASA pushed to 800. Mud and fog helped.

RON DUBICK, SECOND PLACE SPORTS ACTION, THE NEWS-JOURNAL, WILMINGTON, DELAWARE

Sports

Judges of the Pictures of the Year competition are encouraged to choose the best photographs, not simply pictures of the most exciting events. In the category of sports, that is an especially difficult challenge to meet.

When judges view the single entries for only a few seconds, many pictures that depend on subtle detail for their impact are slipped over entirely. (An example of subtlety is the picture of the segregated football players; 216-217)

When so many Americans go red-white and blue crazy over the winnings of the U.S. Hockey Team that defeated the Soviets and Finland for a Gold Medal, it is difficult to evaluate the pictures and not the euphoria we remember experiencing that cold February night.

The year will be remembered for the games played by people like "brat boy" John McEnroe against methodical Bjon Borg who won his fifth straight Wimbledon. And George Brett who's batting average was .390. Americans ran, skied and suffered en masse. Mud wrestling and body building were popular activities. Genuine Risk was the second filly to win the Kentucky Derby and the Phillies of Philadelphia won the World Series and their first world title.

Russian gymnasts were out-of-sync during the opening-day ceremonies for games that many did not play, since President Carter called a U.S. sponsored boycott of the Summer Olympics in Moscow.

People dressed in fancy clothes and white hats to watch polo in West Palm Beach. And everywhere there was football and photographers covering photographers covering football.

In fact, photography is sort of an athletic activity itself. The ideal sports photographer is a little taller, a little stronger (read, "quicker") than the average photojournalist. He carries long, heavy lenses which he can change (and clean) in an instant. He may be a she, in competition for the best position at any athletic event. He or she believes they should have been born with built-in shoulder pads and tire treads on their knees.

Like all successful photojournalists, they are enduring, imaginative, enthusiastic, technically skilled, eager to satisfy their readers with pictures that tell the truth. When a photographer's skill includes coverage of news, feature, illustration, advertising and sports photography, his or her opportunities are greater, influence is sharper and their career years lengthen.

Upsidedown ...
Combined comments from three judges "Terrific photo ... one of a kind timing ... a lucky picture." Mary Schroeder shot just as Green Bay Packer Jim Gueno tried to steal the ball from Billy Sims, (Detroit Lions.) Sims managed to hang onto the ball and the Lions won the game.

Over the top ...
Eagle linebacker Reggie Wilkes broadjumped over a pile of players just as a pass play broke up. The ball bounced around the pile and a fumble was called. "It is difficult to get something different when the entire field seems ringed by the press at football games," said photographer Dennis McDonald.

Through the middle ...
Earl Seubert proved he hadn't lost his timing after 10 years of working the desk and not shooting football. Seubert covered 10 games in one month while photographers at his paper were on strike. "It was good to get back to shooting, even though my old knees burned like fire after each game."

DENNIS MCDONALD, BURLINGTON COUNTY TIMES, MOORESTOWN, NJ

EARL SEUBERT, MINNEAPOLIS TRIBUNE

211

BILL WIPPERT, FIRST PLACE SPORTS FEATURE, BUFFALO
EVENING NEWS

JIM WILEY, WINNIPEG FREE PRESS

DAVE LABELLE, CHANUTE TRIBUNE

What appears to be a dance among referees actually is an argument among those who called the controversial contest between the Buffalo Bills and Baltimore Colts. The Bills were penalized 10 times and lost the game, 17-12. Judges said the picture was "unexpected humor . . . an absolutely funny photograph."

While Dave Labelle photographed the state champions receiving a trophy, he noticed one member of the losing team finding consolation in petting a dog that had wandered onto the field.

After another high school championship loss, a Canadian prep star remained motionless on the bicycle track that outlines the field long after his team members were sent to the showers.

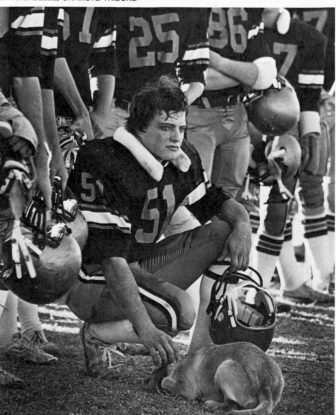

In this picture story produced by Greg Greer, the screams of the cheerleaders, shouts of the coach, and signals exchanged in a huddle are shared in the "quiet zone." The Missouri 1A football team represents the School for the Deaf in Fulton. It is the quietest football team around.

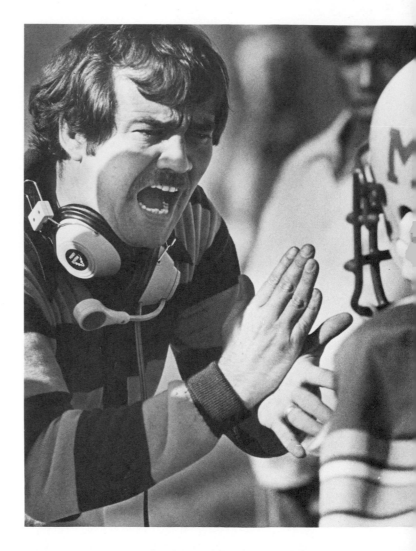

Because it is difficult to "show" silence in pictures, Greer concentrated on the hands of the players, the coach and cheerleaders. It took several tries from under the huddle to get a picture that would tell how each player watched the hands of quarterback Ricky Riedel as he "called" the plays. Among the deaf players, much communication is exchanged by touch. The story was printed in the Columbia Missourian's Sunday magazine.

MICHAEL BRYANT, SAN JOSE MERCURY NEWS

The picture of the football players in a long line along the stadium wall is not what it seems. It is a study in segregation. There are 11 white players on the left and 11 black players on the right. The group was waiting for its turn at the annual press day on the campus of Southern Mississippi University. Michael Bryant found these players dressed as a team but divided among themselves.

At another press-day event, Mark Duncan photographed a freshman player apparently looking for his lost helmet. The picture was made at the University of Dayton after one of the photo sessions.

MARK DUNCAN, ASSOCIATED PRESS

KEN REGAN, CAMERA 5 FOR NEWSWEEK (ORIGINAL IN COLOR)　　　　　DAVID TENENBAUM, ASSOCIATED PRESS

Ken Regan's photo was taken immediately after Mike Erazione's winning shot. Millions of American's shared the joy displayed by the U.S. Hockey Team after its 4-3 win over the Soviet team. The victory stunned the formerly invincible Soviets and sent the U.S. team toward the Gold Medal.

Dave Tennenbaum's photo shows the team's star goalie, Jim Craig, moments after the U.S. won the Gold Medal by defeating Finland, 4-2, in the finals. The success of the U.S. Hockey Team in February of 1980 lifted the spirits of Americans in what was an otherwise bleak winter.

Minnesota's rookie goalie, Don Beaupre stretched to make a save and photographer Richard Olsenius caught the moment. Olsenius used a 180mm lens, 1/500 at f2.8.

Familiar gestures of triumph. And the victory is sweetest when the underdog comes out on top. Kansas State wasn't supposed to win, but did — and upset the Jayhawks in a Big-Eight post-season tournament, giving Tom Reese's picture a little extra importance.

The Generals did not win the lacrosse league championship, but they ended their season by beating the team that did. With crosse in hand, a General tossed a taunting "We're No. 1" sign at his embarrassed foes.

TOM REESE, COLUMBIA MISSOURIAN

LUI K. WONG, RICHARD NEWSPAPERS, INC., VA

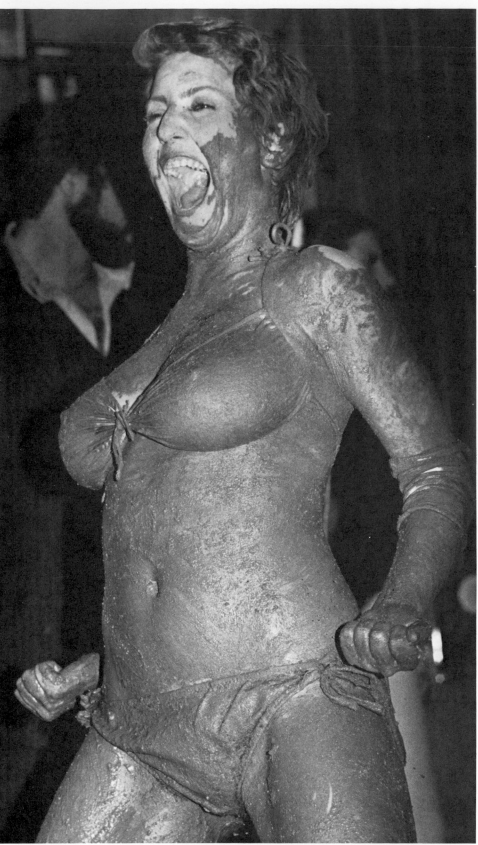

BRUCE HAZELTON, THE DAILY BREEZE, TORRANCE, CA

Several photographers entered pictures of mud wrestling in this year's competition. The caption information they provided indicated the fad was short-lived. Because "upper management felt it was a little too risque for our readership," Bruce Hazelton's picture was not included in the Breeze's feature on mud wrestlers. Hazelton said it took days to clean the mud and grit from his cameras. In this particular California club, the routine included dancing and a strip-tease act along with the mud wrestling.

The sports activity of Eric Heiden is somewhat more lasting than mud wrestling. In Steve Fenn's picture, Heiden exhibits the grace and strength required in speed skating. He was racing toward the first of five Gold Medals that he won at the Lake Placid Winter Olympics. (Original photo in color; Heiden's outfit is a shimmering gold.)

STEVE FENN, ABC SPORTS

Keith Myers capitalized on the Royals logo for strong, graphic composition in this picture of George Brett walking to his position between innings. Brett lead the league in batting average (.390) and the Royals won the American League pennant. (The logo is painted on a grassy slope beyond the outfield wall.)

On his day off, Eric Mencher went out to Spring Training Camp in search of "something unusual." What he found was New York Met's Craig Swan in a flamingo-like pose, practicing his "extended pitching motion." The photo was published the day of the Spring Training strike.

KEITH A. MYERS, UPI, KANSAS CITY, MO

George Steinbrenner, owner of the New York Yankees, throws the photographer a menacing look as he is discovered having a baseball autographed by Howard Cosell. Tom Kasser said when he saw Steinbrenner near the American league dugout, he realized the combination of "the money and the mouth" ... dropped to one knee to get the picture and Steinbrenner gave him a "look that could kill." Instinctively, Kasser shot one more frame. The Yankees' owner took back his ball, handed it to an assistant and stomped off in a disgusted manner. To top it off, the American League lost the All-Star game again that day.

TOM KASSER, SAN BERNARDINO SUN

This collision left both Royal players unable to see clearly. Catcher Darrell Porter lost his glasses and first baseman Willie Aikens found a mitt in his face when they collided while chasing a foul ball.
Keith Myers could see clearly however, from one of the least desirable positions for photographers — behind home plate. The ball dropped and Aikens was given an error.

Double plays in baseball can be the dramatic high point of a game, or just plain funny. Pittsburgh Pirates second baseman Phil Garner rode right over New York Mets Elliott Maddox at second base.
Maddox was moving on a hit by teammate Doug Flynn and broke up the double play at New York's Shea Stadium. Richard Drew titled his picture, "Hopalong Garner."

KEITH A. MYERS, UPI, KANSAS CITY

The famous Wimbledon tiebreaker that lifted Bjorn Borg to his fifth consecutive title also sent challenger John McEnroe to the ground in frustration. Photographer Walter Iooss felt that this shot best exemplified the drama of the match. McEnroe dove for a Borg volley, missed, and continued to lay face down. "The shot I wanted was of McEnroe diving for the volley ... but the aftermath appeared to be the more dramatic moment," said Iooss. The five-set match has been declared one of the greatest ever played.

WALTER IOOSS, JR., SECOND PLACE MAGAZINE SPORTS PICTURE, FOR SPORTS ILLUSTRATED (ORIGINAL IN COLOR)

In what has become a familiar display of temper, McEnroe grimaces at an official's call during the finals of the U.S. National Indoor Championships. The shot was part of a series by Larry Coyne who spent the entire week of the tournament recording McEnroe's volatile behavior. McEnroe became known as much for shooting off his mouth as for smashing balls across the net. With the earned title of "Super Brat," he also earned the distinction of being number two player in the world — behind Borg.

LARRY COYNE, FIRST PLACE SPORTS PICTURE STORY, MEMPHIS PRESS-SCIMITAR

John Zimmerman photographed both Greg Louganis and Jennie Chandler for the May issue of LIFE. This shot of Chandler, an Olympic diver was captured on a single frame by a multiple exposure and strobe technique. Zimmerman draped the diving tower in black to blot out reflections and mounted strobe lights on scaffolds and in aquarium boxes in the pool. The photos were made at night by keeping the shutter open and activating the strobes for each position of the dive. Zimmerman had to quickly refocus to get Chandler's underwater stare.

Greg Smith photographed Louganis as he prepared for his 10-meter dive at the U.S. Outdoor Championships in Bartlesville, Okla. Louganis won the one-, three- and ten-meter events for the second year in a row.

JOHN ZIMMERMAN, THIRD PLACE MAGAZINE SPORTS PICTURE, FOR LIFE MAGAZINE (ORIGINAL IN COLOR)   GREG SMITH, HUTCHINSON (KAN) NEWS

OVERLEAF: The Soviets dominated their own show at the Summer Olympics winning 40 percent of the Gold. They went "head over heels" to sponsor the event but some of the most prestigious guests didn't show up. The United States boycotted the Games to protest Soviet presence in Afghanistan.
The photograph by Heinz Kluetmeier indicates that not everything went off with "split-second precision" at the Moscow Olympics.

HEINZ KLUETMEIER, FIRST PLACE SPORTS, MAGAZINE DIVISION
FOR TIME MAGAZINE (ORIGINAL IN COLOR)

Telekinesis ... the ability to produce movement by mystical powers ... or a golfer attempting to "steer" a ball in a direction it is obviously not going to go. John Hartman photographed the frustration of a game of golf on a windy day when twigs and leaves blow across the green. The upset golfer was playing in the Iowa Junior Girl's tournament near Cedar Rapids.

BRUCE HAZELTON, THE DAILY BREEZE, TORRANCE, CA

Bruce Hazelton tried to show that a woman who sees herself as a "sexy jock" is also a tough competitor on the roller derby track. Darlene Langlois is a Los Angeles roller-derby jammer, a T-Bird star and wants to be portrayed as feminine and lady-like. The picture page in the Daily Breeze shows Langlois applying makeup, dressing for a game, scoring on the track and tearfully nursing a bloody lip. Hazelton considered this one a lucky shot; Langlois was attempting to break free from a taunting competitor.

VICTOR J. WINTER, BARTLESVILLE EXAMINER-ENTERPRISE (OKLAHOMA)

BOB LANGER, CHICAGO SUN-TIMES

A Sooner High School girl's fast-pitch softball team cheers their 15-0 shut-out on their way to the State Championship title in Oklahoma.

A last minute stretch just happened to be the right one for both the photographer and the 28-year-old lawyer who won a 10K road race that she had not even intended to run. Her husband entered her name in the event.

Chicago Hustle coach Bill Gleason gave a lesson in "how to defend against the big girl" just after his prize rookie player, 6'5" Inge Nissen had given him a hug. Nissen is a native of Denmark.

CHARLES W. KNEYSE. THE IDAHO STATESMAN, BOISE, IDAHO

BRAD GRAVERSON, THE NEWS CHRONICLE, THOUSAND OAKS, CALIFORNIA

"Her 5-foot-5 frame, taut 130 pounds and sweet girlish smile make it difficult to believe that this tiny blue-eyed blonde can yank 300 pounds off the floor in a dead lift ... a fifth place at the Women's National Powerlifting Championships ... is testimony to the controlled strength Cameron has built after only 18 months of training." The quote is from a story and picture page layout that Brad Graverson produced for the News Chronicle. (Thousand Oaks, Calif.) Bodybuilding is a family effort in the Cameron home. And mother JoAnne leads the project with husband David as coach and motivator. The two little girls lift weights of their own. When Graverson followed JoAnne through competition, he found little to distinguish her from other female weightlifters.

When he watched her perform as wife and mother, he knew he had the story for an unusual sports feature. He said the story took much more time than he expected to spend, but when an enterprise idea is accepted at the Chronicle, the photographer is responsible for the pictures, text, captions and layout.

BRUCE BISPING, MINNEAPOLIS TRIBUNE

Thousands of Americans continue to drive themselves into condition and gather in large groups to run or ski, hoping to be one of the two or three hundred to finish the race. A worthy objective when the competition is as many as 5,000 fellow athletes.

At least that many skiers eased off the starting line at the Telemark Birkbeiner cross country race and Bruce Bisping was in a position to photograph the mass.

TED BOSWELL, HUDSON DISPATCH

Ted Boswell photographed runners involved in a six-mile race from Fort Lee N. J. to Baker's Field in Manhattan. He titled the photo, "Toll Free."

The objective among many who entered the Marine Corps Marathon in Washington, D.C. was not to win, but to finish. There were runners from 10 to 79 years-old and represented 47 states and 25 countries. In order to capture the motion of the masses, Jim Preston used an 80-200mm zoom at a 30th of a second and depressed the shutter while "zooming" during the exposure. He stood on a bridge and mounted the camera on a tripod. Olympic marathon distance is 26 miles, 385 yards; in this instance those miles were routed past every major landmark in the capitol city. Four of Preston's pictures accompanied a story in the Navy's "All Hands Magazine."

JIM PRESTON, PH1, USN, ALEXANDRIA, VA

More than man against man or man against himself, this race pits man against mountain. The annual Pikes Peak Marathon began at 6,800 feet, climbed to 14,000 and down again. Hornstein said that despite the grueling climb, most runners finished the race — with an exhilarating sense of joy. Judges commented favorably on the fact that this sports picture story was told with only three pictures. The photograph of the lone runner occupied more than 3/4 of a three-board story presentation.

Revisions in the rules for Pictures of the Year, 1981 will permit photographers to use as many as six single boards for story presentations. "Impact" therefore will depend on the content of each photograph rather than the manner in which a series is presented in the "three-board layout."

DON HORNSTEIN, THIRD PLACE SPORTS PICTURE STORY, NEWSPAPER, WALLA-WALLA UNION BULLETIN

Dick Bell's assignment to cover a new polo craze in West Palm Beach turned into more than a routine sports story. "It was a social event, involving every social layer from the men who walked the horses to the men who walked the ladies in designer clothes," he said. Bell was fascinated and "shot like crazy." And his paper published a two-page, full color layout on the event. Bell said, "it was more fun than covering the Super Bowl."

DICK BELL, SECOND PLACE SPORTS PICTURE STORY, NEWSPAPER
ST. PETERSBURG TIMES, (ORIGINAL IN COLOR)

A heavy fog rolled onto the Churchhill Downs track as Bill Luster prepared to photograph horses training for the Kentucky Derby. He could barely see the horses; but after shooting early-morning workouts all week, Luster recognized Genuine Risk by the color of her saddle blanket. He got his picture. Later in the week, Genuine Risk became only the second filly in history to win the Derby. Said Luster, "I'm very fond of the photograph because of the fog, but even fonder of the horse for winning."

BILL LUSTER, THE COURIER-JOURNAL & LOUISVILLE TIMES

Jim Mendenhall spent two and one-half days photographing Kentucky high school all-state runningback George Adams. He followed Adams at school, practice and home for a full-page feature. But Mendenhall got his lead picture on a rainy night while Adams, (33) showed his delight at winning the coin toss. Adams promptly scored four touchdowns in the first half of the game and sat out the second half. At the time the story was published, Adams was the subject of a heavy recruiting campaign from several schools including the University of Alabama.

JIM MENDENHALL, SECOND PLACE SPORTS FEATURE THE COURIER-JOURNAL & LOUISVILLE TIMES

The 38th POY

Judging the Competition

the long days of scrutiny

The Judges:

Ray Mackland

Howard Sochurek

In the upholstered silence of Tucker Forum at the University of Missouri's School of Journalism, five judges pressed buttons to express their feelings for or against the pictures being flipped before them. Three and one half days during the 38th Pictures of the Year competition, a mechanical counter recorded their votes. Click ... click ... "In." Click ... click ... "Out." A voice near the indicator lights on the machine loudly announced each decision. "Out ... out ... out."

In the final heat of each category, student observers shuffled and whispered at the back of the hall, attempting to second-guess the judge's choice of winners. A constant flip-flap of the mat boards against the surface of the showing table made a near-hypnotic sound. One judge yawned. Another chuckled. Two judges argued the merit of a particular choice. Some dramatic stories passed across the table and the room was alive with tension. Necks craned as observers leaned forward in their seats. One series of pictures was recognized as the best entry in the news category. Loud whispers and sighs whisked through the room like leaves blown across a patio. Then there was silence and the judges settled down for viewing the next category.

Seventy student workers flipped pictures or trucked prints from an upstairs room (a borrowed broadcasting lab) to the judging downstairs, then back upstairs again.

Some worked to sort, pack and return prints to photographers. Others helped catalogue those held for possible use in this annual.

And when the judging ended, that work continued. Student coordinator for the 38th POY, Steve Buhman, returned van loads of pictures to their owners and copied the work of the winners for a slide-tape show to be given on Photo Day during Journalism Week in April. A POY print exhibition was prepared and shown the same week.

The competition for 1980 attracted 1,310 photographers and picture editors from across the country. Seventy-seven of them were winners; 176 are represented in "the best of Photojournalism/6." From those 1,310 came 15,000 pictures, many of which had been published in newspapers and magazines throughout the world.

The University of Missouri School of Journalism and the National Press Photographers Association jointly sponsor the POY competition under an education grant from Nikon, Inc. The awards — $12,000 in cash, cameras and trophies — are presented each year on Photojournalism Day during Journalism Week in April.

Judges for 1980 were: Ray Mackland, former photo editor for LIFE; Howard Sochurek, former LIFE Photographer and New York freelancer; Jennifer Coley, director of Gamma-Liaison International News Photo Agency; Dr. John Ahlhauser, photojournalism professor at Indiana University School of Journalism (Bloomington) and Larry Jinks, vice president and editor of the San Jose Mercury-News.

Dr. John Ahlhauser   *Jennifer Coley*   *Larry Jinks*

Judging the last round of the Campaign '80 category ...

The Winners

NEWSPAPER PHOTOGRAPHER OF THE YEAR
George Wedding, San Jose (Calif.) Mercury-News;
Runner-up, Tom Kasser, San Bernardino (Calif.) Sun;
Third place, Bob Thayer, Providence (R.I.) Journal.

MAGAZINE PHOTOGRAPHER OF THE YEAR
Jim Brandenburg, National Geographic; Runner-up, Cary Wolinsky, National Geographic;
Third place, Ted Spiegel, National Geographic.

WORLD UNDERSTANDING AWARD
Bryce Flynn, The Providence (R.I.) Journal, "Warren's Guardian Angel"; Judges' special recognition: David C. Turnley, Detroit Free Press, "Anna & Flander Hamlin: A Lifetime Shared."

FEATURE PICTURE:
First, Jerry Lower, Carbondale Southern Illinoisan, "Passing Time";
Second, Bruce Bisping, Minneapolis Tribune, "Fall Cleaning at Mt. Rushmore";
Third, Jim Wright, Courier-Journal & Louisville Times, "Newlyweds."

SPORTS ACTION:
First, Tom Kasser, San Bernardino (Calif.) Sun, "Another Cowboy Bites the Dust";
Second, Ron Dubick, Wilmington (Del.) News-Journal, "What it is, is Football";
Third, Mary Schroeder, Detroit Free Press, "Haven't We Met."
Honorable mention: Mitsunori Chigita, Associated Press, "Falling at Olympic Ski Jump."

PORTRAIT/PERSONALITY:
First, Michael Wirtz, Dallas Times Herald, "Whatever Happened to Baby Jane";
Second, Bill Wax, Gainesville (Fla.) Sun, "W.J. Cleveland";
Third, Richard Derk, Chicago Sun-Times, "And That's the Way It Is."

PICTORIAL:
First, George Wedding, San Jose Mercury-News, "Floating in the Fog";

NEWS PICTURE STORY:
First, Grant M. Haller, Seattle Post-Intelligencer, "Mt. St. Helens Erupts";
Second, Walter Stricklin, Florida Times-Union & Jacksonville Journal, "A New Life";
Third, Murry H. Sill, Miami Herald, "Miami Riots."
Honorable mention: Joseph Rodriguez, Greensboro (N.C.) News, "Mother Holds Child at Knifepoint."

FEATURE PICTURE STORY:
First, Jay B. Mather, Courier-Journal & Louisville Times, "The Gentle Residents of Casey County";
Second, Gary Parker, Jacksonville Florida Times-Union, "Miracle of Life";
Third, Scott Rutherford, Logan (Utah) Herald Journal, "Marshlands Wildlife.

SPORTS PICTURE STORY:
First, Larry Coyne, Memphis Press-Scimitar, "U.S. Indoor Champion";
Second, Dick Bell, St. Petersburg Times, "Polo";
Third, Don Hornstein, Walla Walla (Wash.) Union-Bulletin, "Men Against the Mountain."

TOM REESE

NEWSPAPER DIVISION

SPOT NEWS:
First, Larry C. Price, Ft. Worth Star-Telegram, Moment of Death";
Second, Jennifer Werner, Kent (Wash.) Fournier Newspapers, "Mt. St. Helens Blows";
Third, George Wedding, San Jose Mercury-News, "Volcano's Deadly Fury."
Honorable mention: Phil Sheffield, Tampa Tribune, "Car on Broken Bridge."

GENERAL NEWS or DOCUMENTARY:
First, Frank Niemeir, Simi Valley (Calif.) Enterpride, "First Solar-Powered Flight";
Second, Tom Kasser, San Bernardino (Calif.) Sun, "The Goose is Loose";
Third, Luciano Mellace, UPI, "Mourn Quake Dead."

CAMPAIGN '80:
First, James Ruebsamen, Santa Monica (Calif.) Evening Outlook, "Intimate Meeting";
Second, Bob Daugherty, Associated Press, "Two Kisses";
Third, George Wilhelm, Simi Valley (Calif.) Enterprise, "It's Cold at the Top."

Second, Erwin Gebhard, Milwaukee Journal, "Thai Road";
Third, Keith Hale, Chicago Sun-Times, "Fishing in the Fog."

FOOD ILLUSTRATION:
First, Fredric Stein, Chicago Sun-Times, "Aged Vinegars";
Second, Roy Scully, Seattle Times, "Glorious Pasta";
Third, Gary Parker, Jacksonville Florida Times-Union, "Popcorn."

FASHION ILLUSTRATION:
First, David Walters, Miami Herald, "Goldie Locks";
Second, Fredric Stein, Chicago Sun-Times, "Country Suits";
Third, Mel McIntire, Dallas Times Herald, untitled

EDITORIAL ILLUSTRATION:
First, Tony Berardi, Chicago Tribune, "Lennon, A Final Tribute";
Second, David Cron, Toledo (Ohio) Blade, "Arson-A City's Curse";
Third, Roberta Burnett, Columbia Missourian, "Peeping Tom."
Honorable mention: Brian Smith, Freelance, "Foreign Students-Caught Between Languages."

MAGAZINE DIVISION

NEWS or DOCUMENTARY:
First, Werner Gartung, Life, "Liberia";
Second, Henri Bureau, Sygma for Time, "Iran, Iraq War";
Third, Peter Marlow, Life, "Workers Triumph in Poland."
Honorable mention: Michael Evans, Time, "Platform Laughter."

FEATURE PICTURE:
First, Patrick Ward, GEO, "English Dance Students at Party";
Second, Joel Meyerowitz, GEO, "St. Louis Arch";
Third, Georg Gerster, GEO, "Burning Strawfield,"
Honorable mention: Ralph Crane, Life, "Strip Mining."

SPORTS PICTURE:
First, Heinz Kluetmeier, Life, "Moscow Olympics";
Second Walter Iooss, Jr., Sports Illustrated, "John McEnroe";
Third, John Zimmerman, Life, "High Art of the Dive."

PORTRAIT/PERSONALITY
First, Neil Leifer, Time, "Bear Bryant";
Second, Richard D. Gordon, Freelance for GEO, "Elderly Catholic Woman in China";
Third, Dennis Brack, Black Star for Time, "Inflationary Headache."

PICTORIAL:
First, Michael E. Keating, Cincinnati Enquirer Magazine,"Morning Mist";
Second, James L. Stanfield, National Georgraphic, "Windsor Castle";
Third, Steve McCurry & Lauren Stockbower, GEO, "Two Camel Herders, Camels & Cigarettes."

SCIENCE/NATURAL HISTORY:
First, Nathan Benn, National Geographic, "Bengal Ballet";
Second, Jim Brandenburg, National Geographic, "Bison in Blizzard";
Third, Bianca Lavies, National Geographic, "Friends?"

NEWS or DOCUMENTARY PICTURE STORY:
First, Patrick Chauvel, Sygma for Newsweek, "aftermath of Archbishop Romero's Funeral";
Second, Mirella Ricciardi, Life, "Gold";
Third, Eve Arnold, Life, "China, Portrait of Change."

FEATURE PICTURE STORY:
First, Mary Ellen Mark, Life, "Mother Teresa";
Second, Jim Brandenburg, National Geographic, "Bamboo";
Third, Reinhart Wolf, GEO, "Japanese Food."
Honorable mention: Ted Spiegel, National Geographic, "A Prayer for Rain in Sand."

EDITING AWARDS

BEST USE OF PHOTOGRAPHS BY A NEWSPAPER
St. Petersburg Evening Independent
St. Petersburg, Florida

NEWSPAPER PICTURE EDITOR
Rick Perry, Seattle Times. Judges' special recognition: Barbara Montgomery, Louisville Courier-Journal.

NEWSPAPER-MAGAZINE PICTURE EDITOR
J. Bruce Baumann, California Today Magazine, San Jose Mercury News. Judges' special recognition: Frederick Ritchin, New York Times Magazine.

BEST USE OF PHOTOGRAPHS BY A MAGAZINE

GEO

MAGAZINE PICTURE EDITOR
Elisabeth Biondi, GEO. Judges' special recognition: Arnold Drapkin, Time. Judges' special recognition for Mt. St. Helens story: Bruce A. McElfresh, National Geographic.

ABOUT THIS BOOK:
Text: 12pt. Century Schoolbook
Captions: 10pt. Optima Italic
Credits: 6pt. Helvetica

Printed on 80lb. dull finish stock
Cover: 10pt. Lustercoat, varnished
Smythe sewn

Printed by Jostens/American
Yearbook Company
Topeka, Kansas

TOM REESE

Acknowledgements:
Ken Cooke served as liaison between the NPPA executive committee, the University of Missouri School of Journalism and numerous potential publishers ...
Angus McDougall reviewed the material as it was prepared for the book and offered continuous encouragement
Joseph L. Hampton ... produced comprehensive layouts for the printer
Jim Balmer ... completed the index to photographers
Wendy Kafoury ... provided assistance with sports information
Steve Buhman ... gathered information and transported pictures from one place to another ...
Tom Reese ... assisted in copying layouts
My family and friends have been patient, enduring and supportive throughout the production of this book. I am deeply thankful to them.

Editor, PJ/6

Index to photographers

JAMES MEEHAN, JOURNAL-COURIER, NEW HAVEN, CT.

BOB MODERSOHN, DES MOINES REGISTER

Melvin Burkhart, 73, is billed as an "anatomical wonder." With a face like Silly Putty and a body with unusual muscular control, Burkhart entertains as a sideshow performer with the James Strates Carnival. Photographer James Meehan asked Burkhart if he could make a face like Popeye. With no hesitation, Burkhart "whipped out his dentures, wiggled his cheeks a bit and presto. became Popeye ..." The picture was made in Burkhart's cramped tent where Meehan hung a piece of black velvet to hide the distractions. The gestures of Burkhart are "the best in the fine tradition of 'girning.'" Friends have told Meehan that the clip of this picture now decorates many of the bathroom and refrigerator doors in New Haven.

An October porch decoration was still holding out but not holding up well in December when Bob Modersohn made his "pooped pumpkin" picture in Ute, Iowa. Elsewhere in this book it is mentioned how people enjoy looking at animals that mimic human expressions. Modersohn's picture reminds us that we can be entertained by vegetables that mimic humans too.